Marketing in the Emerging Markets of Latin America

Also by Marin Marinov

MARKETING IN THE EMERGING MARKETS OF CENTRAL AND EASTERN EUROPE: The Balkans

INTERNATIONALIZATION IN CENTRAL AND EASTERN EUROPE

FOREIGN DIRECT INVESTMENT IN CENTRAL AND EASTERN EUROPE (*with Svetla Marinova*)

Marketing in the Emerging Markets of Latin America

Marin Marinov

First published 2005 by
PALGRAVE MACMILLAN
Houndmills, Basingstoke, Hampshire RG21 6XS and
175 Fifth Avenue, New York, N.Y. 10010
Companies and representatives throughout the world

PALGRAVE MACMILLAN is the global academic imprint of the Palgrave
Macmillan division of St. Martin's Press, LLC and of Palgrave Macmillan Ltd.
Macmillan® is a registered trademark in the United States, United Kingdom
and other countries. Palgrave is a registered trademark in the European
Union and other countries.

ISBN-13: 978–1–4039–4751–2
ISBN-10: 1–4039–4751–1

This book is printed on paper suitable for recycling and made from fully
managed and sustained forest sources.

A catalogue record for this book is available from the British Library.

Library of Congress Cataloging-in-Publication Data
Marinov, Marin, 1948–
    Marketing in the emerging markets of Latin America / by Marin Marinov.
        p.   cm.
    Includes bibliographical references and index.
    ISBN 1–4039–4751–1 (cloth : alk. paper)
    1. Marketing—Latin America—Case studies.   2. Consumers—Latin
America.   I. Title.
    HF5415.12.L3M37 2005
    658.8'0098—dc22   2005048058

10   9   8   7   6   5   4   3   2   1
14   13   12   11   10   09   08   07   06   05

Printed and bound in Great Britain by
Antony Rowe Ltd, Chippenham and Eastbourne

To my wonderful family

Contents

List of Figures

List of Maps

List of Tables

1

Introduction: The Latin American Context

Map 1   Latin America
Source: www.fsmitha.com/h2/map17-la.html.

Brief historical background

Most of the foundations of the contemporary Latin American countries were laid by the ancient Indian civilizations. Some of them – such as the Incas of Peru, the Mayas of Guatemala and southern Mexico and the Aztecs of Mexico – had advanced social, scientific and economic organizations.

The formation of Latin America as a unified region with similar political, economic, social, cultural and demographic characteristics began with the colonization of the region by Spain and Portugal from the end of the fifteenth century. Spanish and Portuguese colonial rule lasted more than 300 years. Most of the Latin American countries won their independence after the revolutions that took place in the first quarter of the nineteenth century. When the region became independent there were attempts to establish a US-style administration across the region but numerous obstacles prevented the formation of a confederation of Latin American states, including the vast size of the intended state, poor infrastructure, substantial socioethnic problems, lack of democratic traditions in government and the strong opposition of the powerful Catholic Church.

The colonial empires of European countries, mostly Spain and Portugal, had a major influence on the political and economic development of the Latin American region from the beginning of the sixteenth century. However this influence started to wane from the middle of the nineteenth century, when most of the Latin American countries became independent.

The struggle for power among the larger states and the fight for national autonomy began immediately after their independence. There were several military conflicts, the most significant of which was the War of the Triple Alliance of 1865–70. Since 1830 Paraguay had been engaged in continuous territorial and trade disputes with its larger and more powerful neighbors, Argentina and Brazil. Similarly Uruguay struggled for independence from Argentina and Brazil. In 1865–70 a war that turned out to be the bloodiest conflict in Latin American military history was fought between Paraguay and the allied countries of Argentina, Brazil and Uruguay. The war brought disaster to Paraguay. Its population was more than halved, two thirds of its male population vanished, more than a quarter of its territory was annexed by Argentina and Brazil, the country was occupied by Argentine and Brazilian troops from 1870 until 1876 and the economy was ruined.

The United States' interest in Latin America took hold in the mid-1850s. It supported Cuba's bid for independence, established political control over Puerto Rico and intervened militarily in Mexico and Nicaragua. Between 1890 and 1930 the United States was the region's largest foreign investor, provider of military aid and trading partner, but for more than 30 years thereafter the US administration maintained a policy of non-interference in Latin America and neglected its economic relationships there. This was reversed at the beginning of the 1960s, when the Soviet Union began to exert a strong ideological and political influence in the region.

In the 1960s and 1970s economic growth averaged 6 per cent in the region and the population increased rapidly. During this period authoritarian military regimes in Chile, Brazil, Argentina and Uruguay enforced bureaucratic measures that were technocratic and repressive. Democracy suffered as political parties and activities were declared illegal, trade unions were repressed and political opponents were killed. At one point in the 1970s, Costa Rica, Colombia and Venezuela were the only countries with civilian governments.

In the late 1970s and the early 1980s the military regimes were replaced by civilian governments. The two principal reasons for this radical change were the total failure of the regimes' economic policies and the strong backing provided by the United States under presidents Carter and Reagan (Hayes, 1988–89). The process continued to spread despite the immense economic hardship and social unrest associated with the transition to democracy.

In the 1980s the return to democracy was accompanied by severe political and economic problems. Investment fell, inflation ran out of control in Brazil, Peru and Nicaragua, unemployment rose and foreign debt skyrocketed. The civilian governments found it difficult to contain this economic volatility and withstand social tensions. They had to adjust their social and political aspirations to the severe limitations imposed by the economic reality and the need to transform their bureaucratic economic systems into efficient and competitive ones became acute. Even the military dictator of Chile, General Pinochet, had to concede the need for some democratic changes. Nonetheless, apart from in Costa Rica, democracy in Central America struggled to make headway. In the Caribbean, democracy in Haiti was suppressed and Cuba was firmly under communist rule.

Geographical location and features

Latin America comprises South America, Central America, the Caribbean islands, and Mexico. Because of their colonial legacy the majority of people speak Portuguese or Spanish. There are also some Francophone countries (for example Haiti and French Guiana), some English-speaking islands and mainland countries (including Jamaica and Belize), and Dutch is spoken in the former Dutch colony of Suriname and a number of Caribbean islands under the jurisdiction of the Netherlands (for example Bonaire and Curaçao). Because of its history of Spanish colonization and large Spanish-speaking population some claim that the south-west of the United States should be considered part of Latin America as well.

Latin America also has a diversity of indigenous languages and religions, and many inhabitants are of African or Asian descent. There are also people of mixed ancestry called *mestizos* and *mulattos*.

The region is geographically diverse, ranging from the high Andes to the Amazonian rainforests and the vast plains of the Pampas. It is also abundant in natural resources and wildlife. The Amazon Basin is rich in timber and a large variety of mineral and other resources. The Basin includes north and central Brazil and large areas of Bolivia, Colombia, Ecuador, Peru, Venezuela and the Guianas (French Guiana, Guyana and Suriname). Economic activities inherited from the colonial past are mining and the production of traditional medicines. The region was rather underdeveloped economically until the early twentieth century, when it became a major supplier of rubber for the booming automotive industry in Europe and the United States. However the importance of the Amazon Basin as a rubber supplier diminished when rubber growing was gradually transferred to Southeast Asian countries, mainly Malaysia.

In the 1970s the Brazilian government implemented a policy to develop the Brazilian Amazon area. The building of a regional transportation infrastructure enabled large-scale illegal deforestation. The rather inefficient and cosmetic response of the Brazilian government to this was to remove some of the tax breaks on regional development, increase central control over logging and proclaim some areas as national parks and nature reserves.

Several of the Amazon parks in Ecuador and Peru have become popular tourist destinations. The Brazilian part of the Amazon Basin is also rich in gold and iron deposits and mining has become a major source of income, attracting migrant workers and a large number of people from the extraction industry. Recently discovered oil deposits in the western part of the basin have sparked boundary conflicts between Brazil, Colombia, Ecuador and Peru, and tensions have arisen between indigenous people in these countries and their central governments.

In Central America agriculture is the main source of export income. Cocoa and indigo have been produced in large quantities since the colonial times, and coffee is important for the economies of Costa Rica, El Salvador and Guatemala. The well-developed agricultural sector has attracted considerable foreign investment, mostly in the production of bananas and other tropical fruit for export. More recently the production of cotton, sugar and beef for export has increased and the drive for economic diversification has resulted in the exportation of farmed shellfish and non-traditional products such as fresh vegetables and flowers.

Multinational corporations (MNCs) have invested heavily in the agricultural development of the region by setting up their own agricultural operations and also contracting out production to local farmers, ensuring a stable income for farmers and quality agricultural products for the MNCs. The low cost of labor in Central America has lured Asian and North American investors into the labor-intensive apparel and shoe manufacturing sectors. Asian businesses have set up production units to reach the highly attractive US consumer market more easily and avoid high transportation costs. Only a few countries in the region have been successful in attracting investment in the high-technology sector. For example in Costa Rica there are businesses that work for Microsoft and Intel. Meanwhile the growth of ecotourism, based on the region's natural beauty and unspoiled coastline and rainforests, has boosted the development of the service sector.

Southern Latin America includes the southern parts of Brazil and Peru and the entire territories of Argentina, Bolivia, Chile, Paraguay and Uruguay. South-east Brazil encompasses the industrial triangle of Belo Horizonte, Rio de Janeiro and São Paulo, which form the backbone of the Brazilian economy. The triangle dates back to the Portuguese colonial past, when the harbor town of Rio de Janeiro was founded. Gold and silver extraction began in the eighteenth century, and extensive coffee production started in the mid-nineteenth century after Brazil gained its independence. After the Second World War the area became an important producer of steel to satisfy domestic needs, particularly in respect of the automotive and aircraft industries.

The Andean region is mostly mountainous and predominantly inhabited by indigenous people working in agriculture and mining. There are numerous natural attractions for tourists but tourism is not well developed. The living standard in rural areas is low, the soil is poor and the climate is cold and dry. Consequently many people migrate to coastal cities and richer neighboring countries. Mining remains the backbone of the regional economies. Chile and Peru rely on copper mining, Bolivia on tin and Colombia on emeralds. Silver and gold are also mined in many countries. However foreign mining corporations control most of the production in the region.

Peru has been transformed by market-oriented economic reforms and privatization. In the 1990s and early 2000s it was successful in bringing about a number of the conditions required for a long-term growth. Banking, retailing, agriculture, mining and manufacturing of consumer goods are the key economic sectors in the country.

The Argentinean economy is based on the utilization of natural resources, the highly educated and skilled workforce, the highly efficient export-oriented agricultural sector and the diversified industrial base. During the last decade the country endured high inflation, a large external debt, a financial crisis and significant budget deficits. However in 2003 Argentina was still the third largest economy in Latin America and enjoyed a relatively high per capita GDP.

Presently Chile has a stable and resilient economy. It has achieved worldwide recognition for its exports of fresh fruit, salmon and wine. Chile's rapid advancement has turned it into a benchmark for other emerging markets engaged in structural reforms, with its sound fiscal and monetary policies, well-developed financial system and adequate market-support infrastructure. Its free-market policies and continuous export growth have turned it into a highly competitive economy and this has been regularly reflected in the country rankings published by independent international organizations.

Together with Chile, Uruguay has one of the most liberal and least corrupt economies in Latin America. In spite of the recent negative economic trends the Uruguayan economy is still performing well in comparison with the other economies in Latin America. It has an export-oriented agricultural sector, a well-educated workforce and high levels of social spending.

The only Latin American country in North America is Mexico, which is rich in history and natural resources. Due to its economic and market significance and its geographic position it is well integrated into regional and global trade.

The Caribbean islands have diverse cultural traditions and political systems, and they include both the poorest and the wealthiest economies in Latin America. The regional cultures are strongly influenced by African traditions and the populations of many Caribbean countries are mainly black. The official languages are Dutch, English, French and Spanish. Millions of Caribbeans also speak Creole. The colonial legacy is still quite strong in that most of the economies continue to rely on agriculture as a main source of export income, with coffee, sugar and tobacco accounting for a major part of export revenue. Some of the countries also raise money from the international sale of mineral and energy resources. For example Jamaica exports bauxite, and Trinidad and Tobago sell oil and gas derivatives. Regional economic cooperation is facilitated by the Caribbean Community and Common Market (CARICOM) and interregional trade accounts for almost 60 per cent of the total value of exports. Tourism and off-shore financial services have contributed substantially to the overall economic development of the Caribbean countries in recent decades.

Economic overview

Prior to European colonization the Incas had established a vibrant civilization with an extensive transportation infrastructure and an advanced sociodemographic organization. The extraction and use of precious metals were well developed.

After the Spanish conquest and until the middle of the nineteenth century Latin America was Europe's most important source of silver. Moreover a large variety of other mineral resources, including oil, were discovered, and millions of African slaves were brought to the region to enable the rapid development of agriculture. By the end of the nineteenth century Argentina had become a significant supplier of agricultural products to the European markets and one of the world's most important exporters of meat. Gradually Brazil and the Caribbean became leading producers and exporters of coffee, hardwood and tobacco.

The economic development of independent Latin America took place in five stages. The first started at different times in different countries, depending on the year of their independence, and continued until the middle of the nineteenth century. On average it lasted 20–25 years. Its major feature was the formation of an independent economic system in each newly created state.

The second stage started in the middle of the nineteenth century and ended at the beginning of the 1930s, when the economic impact of the Great Depression crippled the economies of the region. The exportation of agricultural products and unprocessed natural resources had become the major driving force of economic development, but the world stock market crash of 1929 followed by the global economic crisis caused a sharp decline in exports and a huge reduction of capital inflow into Latin America. These events triggered social turmoil in the region and military regimes forced their way to power to suppress the unrest and enforce order.

The third stage began after the end of the Great Depression and lasted until the end of the 1960s. The two major developments after the 1940s were industrialization and urbanization. This was a time of economic stabilization, driven mostly by inward-looking economic policies based on import substitution and domestic business development. The constant conflicts over land ownership, use and control caused tension in a number of countries. The drive for industrial development was combined with a desire for regional self-sufficiency in order to reduce the domination of the world's great economic powers. This was accompanied by the appearance and practice of numerous political doctrines, ranging from the far right to the far left.

Urbanization on a massive scale began in the 1950s, giving birth to megalopolises such as São Paulo, Rio de Janeiro, Lima and Mexico City. In less than a quarter of a century many towns were turned into some of the largest cities in the world.

Government policies focused on domestic market growth at the expense of exports. Import substitution supported the creation and development of many industries and stimulated the traditionally strong agricultural sector. Population growth and people's increased buying power caused a rise in demand for goods, services, social welfare and health programs, education and transportation, which boosted both economic development and the part played by the state in the planning and regulation of the economy. Prior to the implementation of privatization programs in the late 1980s, in the largest economies of the region – Brazil, Mexico and Argentina – the state owned most of the domestic industries and dominated economic policy making.

Severe economic problems during this period resulted in high inflation. No Latin American currency was convertible and the huge trade deficits that accrued due to the low volume of exports were reflected in enormous foreign debts, mostly to the governments of developed countries. The import substitution policies and protectionist measures implemented by Argentina, Brazil and Mexico impeded the internationalization of domestic industries.

The fourth stage of Latin American economic development took place in the 1970s and 1980s. Despite rising interest rates and mounting debts across Latin America, no national government wanted to abandon the subsidization and protection of domestic industries. Excessive borrowing of ever larger amounts and constantly rising budget deficits meant that national currencies were unrealistically overvalued. By the end of the 1980s Brazil and Mexico had become the largest debtors in the world.

The United States was the largest lender. It not only extended the repayment period for the debts of all Latin American countries but also provided more loans. The largest institutional lender, the International Monetary Fund, agreed to the restructuring of loans provided that the governments in question implemented stabilization and structural adjustment measures for their national economies in general and specific economic sectors in particular. These measures aimed to put inflation under control and stimulate exports, reduce government spending, increase interest rates and restrict salary growth. They also led to the abandonment of subsidies to protect domestic industries, privatization of the majority of government-owned enterprises and the devaluation of all national currencies.

While these measures brought about a fall in inflation and a reduction of debt in most of the Latin American countries, they imposed a huge cost on the economically vulnerable sections of society, led to the closure of many inefficient businesses and ruined entire economic sectors in many of the countries. However privatization and the intro-duction of international market mechanisms gave the region a presence in global markets and prompted an influx of investment capital.

The fifth stage began in the 1990s and was focused on developing a market orientation by means of economic liberalization. Chile was the only exception in this regard as it had begun the process of market liberalization in the mid 1970s.

Thus since the beginning of the 1980s a move towards market orien-tation at the macro- and microeconomic levels has been taking place in all Latin American countries but Cuba, with varying degrees of success. This evolutionary process has created more liberal conditions for business operations and new opportunities for macroeconomic devel-opment. The previous excessive regulation of national economies had hindered the development of international competitiveness by protecting and subsidizing weak and inefficient local industries. Deregulation of the economy to allow market forces to play a major role, the privatiza-tion of productive assets and measures to facilitate international trade have been the most important drivers of change in the region. Latin American counties have opened up to international trade, with an ever growing volume of exports and imports. This has led to an increased inflow of capital into the region and enhanced intraregional capital flows. The telecommunications and transportation infrastructure has been improved in a number of countries.

The regulatory mechanisms imposed by governments have been instrumental in the implementation of evolutionary strategic economic changes throughout Latin America. Policies aimed at curtailing the large national fiscal deficits have been implemented and the money supply has been restrained. Legal systems have been developed and separated from central government functions. The overall effect of political and economic changes has been positive. Macroeconomic stabilization has been achieved and participation in intraregional and global trade has been encouraged.

Apertura, the term used to describe the process of bringing about economic, trade and investment changes, was launched by the Pinochet regime in Chile in the early 1970s. Subsequently other Latin American countries followed suit and by the mid-1980s *apertura* had regional significance. However there was strong opposition to it by opposition groups in most countries. Meanwhile counterbalancing pressures from outside the region had a positive effect on the implementation of measures for economic change.

In 1980–90, on average per capita income fell by about 35 per cent, and in the 1990s it grew by just 2 per cent per year. The social consequences of this were a widening of the income gap and a fall in living standards. In 2003 regional per capita income was 82 per cent of its value in 1980. The most significant macroeconomic achievements of the 1990s were improved fiscal conditions and rigid control over inflation. In 1990–97 the national economies grew moderately (Burki and Perry, 1997), but the large capital inflows and sustainable economic development that were anticipated did not materialize.

The moderate economic growth of 1990–98 was followed by a period of stagnation, and in 2002 high inflation hit some countries, particularly Argentina and Venezuela, with negative economic and social consequences. While there is confidence in the region's future macroeconomic prospects, the anticipated economic growth and consequent improvement in living standards have failed to emerge. Domestic savings and investment have remained low, and labor market volatility, underutilization of the workforce and poor productivity have constrained growth. While domestic investment has fallen, foreign investment has risen, thus making the regional economy largely dependent on foreign capital. This has had a negative impact on the trade balance and economic growth.

In 1990–2003 the average GDP growth rate for Latin America was 2.52 per cent. While GDP growth in Chile, Costa Rica and the Dominican Republic was relatively high at 5.26 per cent, 5.19 per cent and

4.78 per cent respectively, Argentina, Paraguay, Uruguay and Venezuela each recorded less than 2.00 per cent. The most volatile economies were those of Argentina and Venezuela, while the economic performance of Bolivia and Guatemala was relatively uniform. The GDP growth rate of the largest economy, Brazil, was close to the average and there were no significant imbalances.

By the end of 2003 Latin America was home to more than 9 per cent of the global population but it contributed less than 7 per cent of the world's GDP. The ranking of the larger Latin American economies in terms of their total GDP is shown in Table 1.1.

In 2003 the combined GDP of 19 countries in Latin America and the Caribbean amounted to US$1.7 trillion and per capita GDP to US$2619. There were significant differences among countries. Brazil was the largest economy until 2001, when Mexico overtook it by 22.5 per cent. The Mexican economy had been growing much faster than the other economies in Latin America due to the benefits accruing from membership of the North American Free Trade Agreement (NAFTA) and increased investment flows. In 2003 Mexico's GDP reached US$626.1 billion,

Table 1.1 GDP, population size and per capita GDP, Latin America, 2003

	GDP (US$ billion)	Population (millions)	Per capita GDP (US$)
Mexico	626.1	106.2	5895
Brazil	497.9	179.1	2783
Argentina	129.7	37.9	3422
Venezuela	84.9	26.2	3242
Colombia	77.8	45.3	1718
Chile	72.1	16.0	4512
Peru	60.6	27.5	2205
Ecuador	27.1	13.4	2135
Guatemala	19.5	12.7	1535
Costa Rica	17.6	4.2	4190
Dominican Republic	16.0	8.8	1823
El Salvador	13.1	6.7	1957
Panama	12.9	3.2	4035
Uruguay	11.2	3.4	3296
Bolivia	8.6	8.8	978
Honduras	6.9	7.0	783
Paraguay	5.8	6.0	967
Haiti	3.9	8.1	482
Nicaragua	2.6	5.6	466

Sources: IMF (2004); Population Reference Bureau (2004); *Latin Business Chronicle* (2004).

25.7 per cent higher than that of Brazil. Argentina and Venezuela ranked third and fourth respectively. Colombia, despite political and economic volatility, ranked fifth. Chile was the sixth largest economy, benefiting from years of economic stability and sustainable growth. However in general the GDP growth rates in Latin America were rather low in comparison with those in other emerging markets, such as China, Russia, India, Central and Eastern Europe, and Sub-Saharan Africa.

In 2002 Latin America had experienced its most substantial economic downturn since the beginning of the 1980s, with real GDP falling by more than 0.25 per cent. The most substantial recessions had been experienced by Argentina and Venezuela, while in Chile the downturn had been insignificant and the Peruvian economy had grown by more than 5 per cent.

In 2003, average per capita GDP in the region was US$3580, with Mexico ranking first and Chile second. Per capita GDP in Brazil was relatively low compared with the size of its economy, while Panama ranked thirteenth in terms of its economy but third in terms of per capita GDP. When compared with other developing regions, Latin America's per capita GDP performance was not encouraging (Table. 1.2).

Table 1.2 Average annual percentage change of real per capita GDP, developing regions, 1998–2003

	Average annual change of real GDP per capita (%)
Developing regions worldwide (excluding Latin America)	3.3
Asia	4.8
Central and Eastern Europe	2.6
Middle East	1.8
Sub-Saharan Africa	0.6
Latin America	–0.1
Mexico	1.3
Chile	1.1
Peru	0.3
Brazil	0.0
Ecuador	–0.3
Colombia	–0.9
Argentina	–2.6
Uruguay	–2.7
Venezuela	–4.9

Sources: Author's own calculations based on IMF and World Bank data.

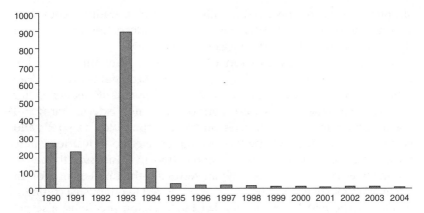

Figure 1.1 Average annual inflation, Latin America, 1990–2004 (per cent)
Source: Adapted from www.latin-focus.com.

However in 2004 Latin America performed better than expected and GDP was on the rise. The GDP of the six largest economies grew by more than 3 per cent. This growth was supported by a high external demand for exports, mostly commodities but also some manufactured goods. Export growth spurred domestic investment, and an increase in real wages had a positive effect on consumption.

The predictions for GDP growth in 2005–6 are optimistic: the United Nations Economic Commission for Latin America and the Caribbean (ECLAC) and the IMF predict rises of 4.5 per cent in 2005 and 3.9 per cent in 2006. However there have been warnings that the forecast rates have been overestimated in order to encourage borrowing. On occasion economic instability, restructuring and slow growth have resulted in relatively high inflation. While Argentina and Brazil have managed to restrict inflation to single-digit figures, Venezuela has found it difficult to keep it below 20–30 per cent. Nonetheless on average inflation has been under control in Latin America since the mid 1990s (Figure 1.1).

Latin American economic integration

There have been numerous attempts to integrate economic activities in Latin America. The formation of a Latin American Free Trade Association was first discussed in the 1950s and was initiated in 1961. The original aim was to establish a free trade area by the beginning of the 1970s, but due to the serious economic problems and protectionist policies of the Latin American governments the attempt was unsuccessful, although not abandoned. Meanwhile two regional trading blocs were set up: the Andean Pact, later renamed the Andean Community, and the Latin American Integration Association (ALADI).

The Andean Pact was signed in 1968 by Bolivia, Colombia, Ecuador, Peru and Venezuela and was the first relatively successful Latin American regional grouping. The principal measures were a tariff reduction for international trade, the establishment of a common external tariff and the introduction of joint policies on the transportation of goods and economic cooperation in the functioning of selected industries. These measures facilitated government intervention in business activities in the member countries but somewhat restricted the implementation of free market mechanisms. The members intended to establish a common market by the mid-1990s, but market liberalization problems, a severe recession in the late 1990s and distrust between the member states impeded this objective. Hence the organization continues to function as a customs union but the individual states are tending to seek bilateral agreements with non-member countries.

ALADI was formed in 1980 and was largely based on preferential tariff agreements between pairs of similarly developed member states. This led to more than 20 bilateral agreements and five subregional pacts, but economic cooperation and free trade between the member states failed to develop and consequently some of its members withdrew to form the Southern Common Market (MERCOSUR).

MERCOSUR was created by Argentina and Brazil in 1988 and expanded in 1991 to include Paraguay and Uruguay. Its foundation was preceded by 17 bilateral agreements between Argentina and Brazil in 1984–88 to improve conditions for international trade. In 1996 Bolivia and Chile joined MERCOSUR as associate members. The largest economic bloc in Latin America, MERCOSUR still operates as a customs union but aspires to become a common market in the near future. The member states account for almost two thirds of the total Latin American economic output and the combined market consists of more than 230 million people. There is a high degree of economic unification among the member states. They have an open policy towards foreign direct investment but somewhat restrictive regulations on international trade. Brazil and Argentina have attracted the bulk of foreign direct investment. Brazil is the largest, richest in terms of natural resources and most influential economy in the bloc. Argentina has the largest middle class but has recently suffered from economic volatility.

Within the bloc there are both integrative and divergent forces. For example there are differing perspectives on the desired level and scope of economic integration as well as on protectionist measures that limit the degree of freedom to conduct international trade. This has had a negative impact on international competitiveness at the firm, industry, national and regional levels and limited the bargaining power of MERCOSUR *vis-à-vis* other powerful economic blocs. The ambition of the member states is to incorporate all the other Latin American countries but Cuba and turn MERCOSUR into a Free Trade Area of the Americas. However negotiations have been hampered by opposition from strong social movements.

Latin America is very attractive to US and European companies, mostly because of its markets but also as a possible low-cost production base. Numerous European companies have established themselves in the region due to a common historical background and cultural affinity. Many of these businesses have penetrated the MERCOSUR markets and operate as local companies with local supply chains, product development and managerial autonomy. However Canadian and US companies have been pressing hard for faster integration, which would challenge the European companies entrenched in the region. The MERCOSUR bloc has also attracted quite a few highly competitive Japanese investments based on a strategic approach to the region.

The Central American Common Market (CACM) was set up in 1960 by El Salvador, Guatemala, Honduras and Nicaragua, and it was later joined by Costa Rica. In the early stages of its development the CACM concentrated on economic integration. Further development has been hampered by the competitive rather than complementary nature of the economies of the member countries and political and military conflicts.

The Caribbean Community and Common Market (CARICOM) facilitates trade cooperation in the Caribbean. It was formed in 1973, has a market of almost six million people and a combined GDP of around US$30 billion. Although the ultimate purpose of CARICOM is to establish a common market, the process has been deterred by historical trade realities and resource scarcity, resulting in a higher volume of trade with non-member countries.

The introduction of free trade in most countries has had a positive effect on the internationalization of the national economies. Mexico benefited hugely from joining NAFTA in 1994, thereby intensifying its trade cooperation with the United States and Canada. Chile is a prime candidate for an expanded NAFTA. It has recently signed a free trade agreement with the United States, following similar agreements with Canada and Mexico. The Chilean economy has been the fourth fastest growing one in the world over the last decade thanks to the government's

Table 1.3 Characteristics of the principal Latin American economic blocs

	Type of agreement	Member countries	Population in 1999 (millions)	GDP per capita in 1999 (US$)	Total GDP in 1999 (US$ billion)	Intra-bloc exports in 2000 (US$ billion and percentage of total)	Exports to Latin America in 2000 (US$ billion and percentage of total)	Total exports in 2000 (US$ billion)	Main export countries
NAFTA	Free trade area	Canada, Mexico, United States	404	21 186	8570.0	702.0 (57.0)	177.8 (14.0)	1240.0	United States, Canada, Mexico
CACM	Customs union	Costa Rica, El Salvador, Guatemala, Honduras, Nicaragua	32	1 162	37.7	2.5 (22.0)	3.2 (28.0)	11.7	Guatemala, El Salvador, Costa Rica
Andean Community	Customs union	Bolivia, Colombia, Ecuador, Peru, Venezuela	111	1 969	218.6	5.1 (8.6)	12.5 (21.0)	59.2	Venezuela, Colombia, Peru
MERCOSUR	Customs union, from 2005 common market	Argentina, Brazil, Paraguay, Uruguay. Associate members: Bolivia and Chile	213	3 710	791.0	18.3 (21.0)	28.9 (35.5)	86.4	Argentina, Brazil

Source: Adapted from McCoy (2001).

market liberalization efforts, which have stabilized the economy, kept down inflation and encouraged a strong financial system. The other economic blocs have had varying degrees of success in dismantling tariff and trade barriers and encouraging the free trade of goods. A summary of the main characteristics of the principal blocs is presented in Table 1.3.

Many free trade agreements have been established between individual Latin American countries and regional blocs in other parts of the world, including one between Mexico and the European Union (EU) and a planned collaboration between MERCOSUR and the EU for pan-Atlantic free trade.

Internationalization

Internationalization of the business operations of Latin American companies started in the 1830s, but until the end of the Second World War it was on a limited scale. A new era of internationalization started in the 1970s, with imports of goods and services, know-how transfer and capital inflow being counterbalanced by exports, contractual business arrangements and significant flows of capital within the region and to other parts of the world. Large Latin American companies have entered into strategic alliances with one another and with companies from the developed world. For example the Colombian dairy product company Alpina has entered into a strategic marketing alliance with the Venezuelan meat processing firm Plumrose, whereby they share knowledge of their home markets and provide access to their distribution networks and retail outlets (Gómez, 1997). Companies in industries such as oil (Venezuela), cement (Mexico), steel (Brazil, Chile, Argentina and Mexico) and copper (Chile) have expanded their operations across Latin America and beyond, reaching out to North America, Europe and Asia.

Internationalization has been uneven among countries and has undergone ups and downs. The annual export growth in the region in 1990–2000 was 9 per cent, mostly due to the strong growth of Mexican exports.

Manufactured exports from Mexico, Central America and the Caribbean tend to be made from imported inputs. This is the so called *maquila* system, which is based on foreign direct investment and has made the countries in question partners in multinational integrated production. The principal destination for these exports is the United States. Manufactured exports are supplemented by traditional agricultural exports. In Central America the latter have undergone substantial diversification.

Exports from South America to other parts of the world are dominated by commodities and natural resources, a small percentage of which have been subject to some value-adding activity. Intraregional trade is highly diversified and includes capital-intensive manufactured goods. Most of the foreign direct investment (FDI) in the region is associated with natural resources or is motivated by market access. The labor-intensive industries also attract some FDI, whereas FDI in technology-intensive manufacturing is small and goes mainly to Brazil.

Some of the economic problems in Latin America stem from the discrepancy between GDP growth and export activities. While exports have grown, the involvement of local companies in domestic production and value-adding activities has fallen as a result of FDI and the outsourcing activities of large multinationals that use Latin America as a cheap production base. This has hindered the expansion of domestically oriented production and had a negative effect on overall regional economic growth. It might be thought that countries whose exports mainly consist of natural resources stand a better chance of expanding their domestic businesses than those involved in international supply chains. However, natural resource extraction is dominated by foreign investors.

The countries that have managed to achieve significant GDP growth have also increased their exports, including Chile, the Dominican Republic and Costa Rica. In contrast Brazil, Venezuela, Colombia and Ecuador have had low GDP growth rates and only small rises in exports, and Paraguay's low GDP growth rate has been accompanied by negative export growth.

European MNCs, mainly Spanish, have invested in telecommunications, energy infrastructure and finance, especially in the MERCOSUR countries and Chile. The interest of large MNCs in this part of the world is largely associated with the region's colonial past and the deregulation, liberalization and privatization of the sectors in question. However the inflow of FDI has had a limited effect on the competitiveness of these economies as it has been mostly concentrated in services and infrastructural improvements, rather than involving technological transfer and innovation. FDI in natural resource extraction has mostly gone to the Andean region, Chile and Argentina, which have high-quality natural resources such as oil, natural gas, copper and gold.

The bulk of FDI in Mexico, Central America and the Caribbean countries is used to establish production facilities to exploit the relatively cheap labor, thus serving as export platforms and links in international supply chains. MNCs from the United States have established low-cost assembly operations for the automotive and electronics industries, plus production facilities in labor-intensive industries such as apparel. The proximity of these markets to the vast North American consumer base allows US companies to reduce their production costs and easily transport the final goods to US markets. Mexico has preferential access to the North American market by way of NAFTA, while many Caribbean countries have access to the US market via the United States–Caribbean Basin Trade Partnership Act (CBTPA). Two thirds of the value of Latin American trade and almost three quarters of investment flows are associated with North American activities, mostly those of the United States.

The current share of Latin American exports and imports in total international trade is approximately 5 per cent. The most export-oriented countries are Mexico and Brazil. Mexican exports account for more than 40 per cent of the total value of Latin American exports and Brazilian exports for about 17 per cent. Latin American countries have been eager to increase their volume of exports and achieve a positive trade balance. Their efforts were rewarded in 2003–4, when the region achieved a trade surplus for the first time in 50 years (Figure 1.2).

The economic structure of Latin American countries has been substantially changed by foreign investment in those countries which have improved the international competitiveness of certain sectors (Table 1.4). The largest recipients of FDI are Brazil and Mexico. Investment is skewed towards services, although Argentina has received major

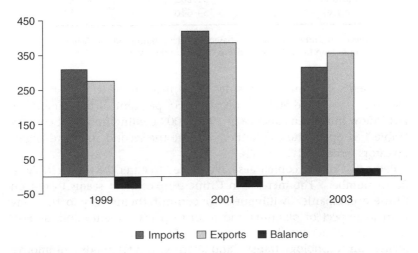

Figure 1.2 Latin American imports, exports and trade balance, 1999–2003 (€ billion)
Source: http://trade-info.cec.eu.int/.

Table 1.4   Cumulative inflow of FDI into the largest Latin American economies, 1996–2003

Country/Sector	Cumulative FDI (US$ million)	Share (%)
Argentina	60 747	100
Primary	25 934	43
Manufacturing	11 314	19
Services	18 756	31
Other	4 743	8
Brazil	157 468	100
Primary	6 469	4
Manufacturing	37 734	24
Services	113 258	72
Chile	36 467	100
Primary	10 098	28
Manufacturing	4 105	11
Services	22 264	61
Colombia	20 663	100
Primary	3 966	19
Manufacturing	3 710	18
Services	12 987	63
Mexico	106 998	100
Primary	1 090	1
Manufacturing	51 262	48
Services	54 646	51

Source: Author's calculations based on data published by Economic Commission for Latin America and Caribbean (ECLAC).

investments in primary industries. The major provider of FDI in the region is the United States, with about 55 per cent of the cumulative FDI inflow into Latin America in 1996–2003 coming from that country (Table 1.5). Spain and the Netherlands are the second and third largest investors respectively.

Recently Chinese companies have started to enter the region in significant numbers. The increase in Chinese investment seems to rest on Chinese companies' willingness to commit themselves to the long term in respect of planning and return on investment. Chinese FDI, which sometimes involves reverse trade from Latin America to China, focuses on technology transfer and sharing, capital goods, automotive products, electronic components, timber and wood products, transgenic

Table 1.5 FDI from the three major investing countries in the largest Latin American economies, 1996–2003

Recipient/investor	Cumulative FDI (US$ million)	Percentage share of total
Argentina: total FDI	60 747	100
Spain	26 020	43
United States	7 552	12
The Netherlands	5 926	10
Total	39 498	65
Brazil: total FDI	157 468	100
United States	33 998	22
Spain	25 612	17
The Netherlands	16 332	11
Total	75 942	50
Chile: total FDI	36 467	100
United States	9 613	25
Spain	8 871	24
Canada	5 155	14
Total	23 639	63
Colombia: total FDI	20 663	100
Spain	2 882	14
United States	2 592	13
The Netherlands	1 498	7
Total	6 972	34
Mexico: total FDI	106 998	100
United States	70 579	66
The Netherlands	9 693	9
Spain	6 068	6
Total	86 340	83

Source: Author's calculations based on data published by Economic Commission for Latin America and Caribbean (ECLAC).

seeds, food processing, mining and distribution. Chinese companies are also interested in importing natural resources from Latin America. The countries with the largest Chinese presence are Brazil, Chile, Mexico, Venezuela, Argentina and Colombia. About 36.5 per cent (US$1.04 billion) of China's outward FDI in 2003 flowed into Latin America (www.china.org.cn).

FDI rose until 1999, but between 1999 and 2003 it plummeted from US$108.3 billion to US$42.3 billion (United Nations, 2004) (Figure 1.3). Investment in the Caribbean increased slightly but that

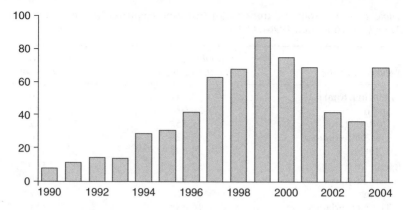

Figure 1.3 Annual net FDI inflows, Latin America, 1990–2004 (US$ billion)
Sources: Economic Commission for Latin America and Caribbean (ECLAC); IMF Balance of Payments Statistics.

in the MERCOSUR countries fell fourfold. Hardest hit by this negative trend were Paraguay, with a fall of 75 per cent in 2001–2, and Argentina, with a fourteenfold decrease between 2000 and 2002. While Mexico and Brazil also suffered a fall in FDI they retained their top position (Figure 1.4). The uneven economic development and varying resources of the region's countries, coupled with the growing attraction of Mexico as a production base within NAFTA, were important factors in this trend. The FDI lost to the Latin American countries was mostly diverted to Southeast Asia.

The situation improved in 2003–4, when FDI rose by 37 per cent to US$69 billion. The factors that facilitated this increase were relative economic stability and conductive policies. In 2004 Mexico and Brazil attracted about 50 per cent of the volume of FDI, followed by Chile, Venezuela and Argentina. However FDI flows to the region remained lower than those to China and elsewhere in Asia (Figure 1.5).

The United States and Spain are expected to remain the major providers of FDI. It is predicted that in 2005–8 Brazil, Mexico, Argentina, Chile, Venezuela, Peru and Colombia will attract about 80 per cent of the overall regional inflow. The three major industries – primary (agriculture, petroleum extraction and mining), manufacturing (rubber and plastic products, electronics, textiles and apparel, and automotive products) and services (hospitality, wholesaling and retailing, tourism, financial services and transportation) – will continue to attract the bulk of FDI. The major mode of market entry in the coming years will shift from

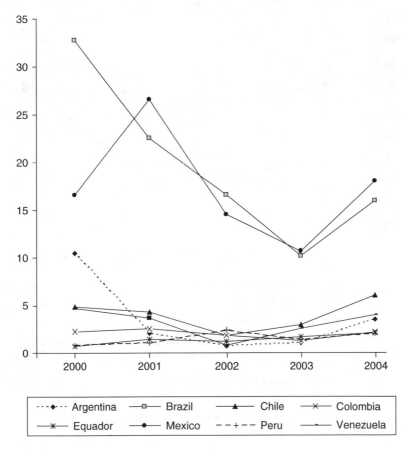

Figure 1.4 Annual net FDI inflows, largest Latin American economies, 2000–4 (US$ billion)
Sources: Economic Commission for Latin America and Caribbean (ECLAC); IMF Balance of Payments Statistics.

mergers and acquisitions to greenfield investments, followed by strategic alliances and international joint ventures, mostly with local partners. More than 75 per cent of FDI in Latin America in 2005–8 is expected to go into production, distribution and infrastructural development, while the volume of investment in R&D is likely to be rather small. This may create some problems for the future international competitiveness of Latin American industries and companies as innovation and technology transfer will be slow and will lag behind developments in other emerging markets such as China.

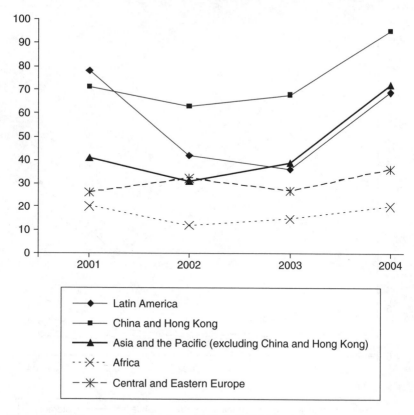

Figure 1.5   FDI in emerging markets, 2000–4 (US$ billion)
Source: UNCTAD (www.unctad/fdistatistics).

Intraregional investment

Intraregional investment has been aided by a number of factors, including the reduction or elimination of restrictions on foreign capital, privatization programs, advances in regional integration, strategic alliances between companies from different countries, and new strategies for market penetration, including the establishment of manufacturing enterprises and the acquisition of local competitors.

The leading intraregional investing countries are Chile, Mexico and Argentina. Intraregional investment is particularly strong in the Southern Cone, which encompasses the MERCOSUR member states plus Chile, Bolivia and Peru. Chilean firms are leading the internationalization process throughout Latin America, while Mexican enterprises are investing in Central America and some South American economies

(Argentina, Chile, Colombia and Venezuela). There is also some investment flow between Colombian and Venezuelan companies.

Outward FDI

Latin American companies have invested in many countries of the world, particularly the United States. In the case of the latter the most active investors have been Mexico, Venezuela and Panama. Latin American companies use a variety of modes of market entry into the United States, including acquisitions, international joint ventures, greenfield investments and strategic alliances. They focus mostly on the manufacture of industrial and consumer goods, followed by financial services and trade. By 2001 cumulative Latin American FDI in the United States accounted for 4.5 per cent of the total cumulative foreign investment in the country (Vasquez-Parraga *et al.*, 2004). Latin American FDI in China has also increased substantially, and by the end of 2003 it had reached US$30 billion. At the end of 2002 Latin American FDI in the European Union (EU) accounted for 0.9 per cent of the EU's total FDI

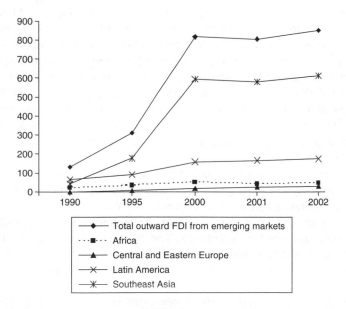

Figure 1.6 Cumulative outward FDI from emerging markets, 1990–2002 (US$ billion)
Source: UNCTAD.

stock, while about 11 per cent of the EU's outflow went to Latin America. Outward FDI from emerging markets has been increasing since the early 1990s, particularly in the case of Southeast Asia and Latin America (Figure 1.6).

Market potential

Latin American countries have a significant market potential when measured by the size of the population and the opportunities for market development. Cavusgil (1997) offers a methodology for evaluating the potential of emerging markets, based on their size, growth rate, market intensity, consumption capacity, receptivity, commercial infrastructure, economic freedom and country risk. The results of an application of his methodology to the market conditions of the largest Latin American economies are presented in Table 1.6.

Chile has the largest market potential as it has the most liberal market conditions of all emerging markets, its country risk is the lowest in Latin America and it has the most developed commercial infrastructure in the region. Mexico has the second largest market potential thanks to the high market intensity of the Mexican economy and the relatively large degree of economic freedom. Nevertheless Chile and Mexico rank behind the most advanced of the former communist countries in Central Europe, namely Hungary and the Czech Republic (which respectively have the sixth and seventh highest market potential indices among emerging markets worldwide because of their highly developed commercial infrastructure, consumption capacity and economic freedom) and Poland (which ranks ninth because of its large consumption capacity, economic freedom and high market intensity).

Argentina ranks third in market potential in Latin America. It has a high market growth rate and market intensity, but it is perceived as the riskiest emerging market in the world. With a relatively high market growth rate and economic freedom, Brazil ranks fourth despite its extremely low market receptivity. The Peruvian market is similar in size to that of Chile and has recently achieved high growth, market intensity and economic freedom, which puts it fifth in terms of market potential.

The market potential of these countries should encourage foreign investors to develop new or penetrate existing market segments. However the low purchasing power of the majority of the population

Table 1.6 Ranking of large Latin American economies according to market potential, 2004

	Market size	Market growth	Market intensity	Market consumption capacity	Commercial infrastructure	Economic freedom	Country risk	Market receptivity	Overall market potential index	World ranking	Ranking in Latin America
Chile	2	78	56	13	54	100	57	11	45	10	1
Mexico	13	61	66	27	37	66	50	23	44	11	2
Argentina	5	84	55	39	41	52	1	3	29	19	3
Brazil	26	58	38	13	38	56	25	1	28	20	4
Peru	2	62	62	53	15	62	20	2	27	21	5
Colombia	4	51	52	17	32	39	23	5	16	23	6

Note: The value of the measures for various countries is between 1 and 100, in accordance with the system developed by Cavusgil (1997).

will require companies to redefine the value–price–performance relationship in order to achieve market growth.

Consumer patterns

The population of Latin America has increased more than fivefold over the past century, reaching 550 million by the end of 2004. The most populated countries are Brazil and Mexico, which account for more than 50 per cent of the total population. Consumers in Argentina, Brazil, Chile, Colombia, Mexico and Venezuela are highly receptive to a diverse array of goods, ranging from computer equipment and cars to food, beverages and health-care products.

Over the last 50 years there has been considerable urbanization, and in Argentina, Chile, Uruguay and Venezuela the urban population now accounts for more than 90 per cent of the total. Some of the world's largest metropolitan areas are in Brazil (São Paulo and Rio de Janeiro), Mexico (Mexico City) and Argentina (Buenos Aires), with more than 65 million inhabitants.

Since the late 1950s strong social movements have brought about radical social changes and empowered Latin American women. The movement for ethnic and racial equality changed the social positions of indigenous, mestizo, mulatto and black people, while the Catholic Church, challenged by evangelical Protestant sects and religions of African origin, has attempted to reinforce the role of Catholicism in society by empowering the poor.

The highest average pretax incomes in Latin America (above US$15 000 per annum) are earned in the Bahamas, Barbados and Puerto Rico, and the lowest (below US$2500 a year) are earned in Bolivia, Haiti and Honduras. There are five major socioeconomic classes in Latin America, ranging from A to E. The number of rich people in class A (average monthly household income of US$3000) and well-off people in class B (US$900 per month) has recently diminished. These groups we currently estimated to make up about 10 per cent of the total Latin American population. The size of class C (medium-income earners with an average monthly household income of US$350) has stayed relatively the same at about 20 per cent. Those in classes D (poor) and E (very poor), whose combined average monthly household income is US$100, presently account for some 70 per cent of the population. Table 1.7 shows the population distribution of these classes and their buying power in the two most populous countries of the region – Brazil and Mexico.

Table 1.7 Buying power of consumers in classes A to E, 2003

	Latin America	Brazil	Mexico
Class A			
Percentage of population	2	3	2
Percentage of buying power	22	30	19
Class B			
Percentage of population	8	16	11
Percentage of buying power	27	34	34
Class C			
Percentage of population	20	29	23
Percentage of buying power	26	25	28
Classes D and E			
Percentage of population	70	52	64
Percentage of buying power	25	11	20

Sources: Strategy Research Corporation; UN *Demographic Yearbook*; UNESCO *Statistical Yearbook*.

Class C consumers have developed a number of common characteristics in almost all countries, suggesting that the effect of national
culture on their buying behavior has reduced significantly. Referred to
by Ruiz-Velasco (1996) as the 'new consumers' of Latin America, they
prefer to shop at large, mostly foreign, retail outlets such as Carrefour
and Wal-Mart. Class D and E consumers are less affected by the convergence of cultural trends that have influenced classes A, B and C. Class D
workers are concentrated in the grey economy, which in some countries
provides work for more than 50 per cent of the labor force. Class E
people are temporarily employed or have been redundant for long
periods of time, and have to survive on less than US$20 a month.
According to official statistics more than two fifths of the regional
population live in poverty, and in some countries poor people account
for up to 90 per cent of their total population. The share of the population
living in poverty is highest in the Central American countries, but in
absolute numbers tens of millions of poor people live in Argentina,
Brazil and Mexico.

Most consumers have a generally positive attitude towards foreign
products (Sharma, 2002). However as income disparities are large in the
region the purchasers tend to be middle-class consumers who are highly
selective in their buying behavior, with a proclivity for brand switching
and specific requirements in respect of value for money. According to
Prahalad and Lieberthal (1998), such consumers are more sensitive to
the price-performance equation than their counterparts in the United

States and are willing to pay a premium for products that offer more functional features than similar products sold in the same market. Moreover they tend to shun outdated products marketed by multinational companies with the intention of exploiting their residual value (ibid.), and ethnocentrism can result in the preferential purchase of local or regional products. Hence foreign companies need to adapt their marketing campaigns accordingly and offer consumers more customized products than those manufactured by local companies.

In Latin America the specific meanings of value, functionality and price can differ from those in developed market economies. A study by Carramengha *et al.* (1999) of consumers' perceptions of the value of global brands shows that in Argentina, Brazil, Chile and Colombia the most important factors for consumers are warranty, resale value, styling and exterior design. In the automobile market Ford has the highest consumer-defined brand equity, followed by Chevrolet and Mercedes Benz. However there are differences between countries. Argentines prefer Ford, Renault and Peugeot; Brazilians like Volkswagen, Chevrolet and Fiat; Chileans mostly buy Mercedes Benz, Ford and Chevrolet; and Colombians prefer BMW, Citroen and Ford. This indicates that a single positioning strategy for all four markets cannot guarantee success.

Research on Latin American consumers carried out by the British media group WPP in 2003 found that consumers who expressed animosity towards the United States could still be positive about US brands. Replication of the study in 2004 revealed that consumers in the region – and particularly in Argentina, Brazil, Chile and Mexico – had a higher degree of resistance to US brands. This attitude was mostly associated with younger people (Roberts, 2004).

On the one hand the difficulties that Latin American companies have had with preserving their market positions and withstanding competitive pressure by American MNCs have made consumers more sensitive to the origin of the products they buy. On the other hand the higher quality or price competitiveness of some European and US products and brands have proven attractive to consumers. In general Latin American consumers have high uncertainty avoidance in purchasing high and low involvement products. Word-of-mouth recommendation by friends and family is an important feature of consumer behavior patterns in the region, as all countries score comparatively high in collectivism. This is particularly the case with high value purchases of consumer durables.

According to Cramphorn and Caldeiro (1999), people's reaction to advertisements in Argentina and Brazil is rather similar to that in Spain and Portugal in terms of evaluating the creativity and brand associated content of advertisements. They suggest that advertisements used in Spain and Portugal could be easily transferred to Argentina and Brazil. Mexicans are highly receptive to US advertisements and have a generally positive attitude towards Spanish advertisements for up-market products and services. Aspirational advertisements are more popular with class A and B consumers than informative ones. The majority of class D and E consumers throughout Latin America are little influenced by advertisements in their consumption habits which are restricted by extreme price sensitivity.

Retailing

In Latin America retailing has undergone significant changes in the last 20 years, although food retailing has preserved its traditional format, with four distinct types of retail outlet. The first consists of a huge number of independent outlets that range from open-air stalls to small conventional shops selling a wide variety of food product lines or specializing in particular categories of food. The second group of food retailers sell fresh food and/or fast moving consumer goods in open-air or covered outlets mainly in the larger urban areas. In areas with smaller populations these retailers move their operations from one area to another on a regular basis. The third type of retail outlet consists of independently run large shops or chains offering a variety of products. Finally there are chains of supermarkets and hypermarkets.

The market share of super- and hypermarkets has increased significantly during the last decade, and on average they accounted for 60 per cent of the value of food sold in the whole of Latin America in 2001 (Reardon and Berdegué, 2002). Due to quick consolidation and foreign acquisition or greenfield investment in retailing the market share of the largest outlets, most of them with foreign ownership, is as shown in Table 1.8.

In Brazil the market leader is the Brazilian group Pão de Açúcar, which has dominated the market for decades. It is followed by Carrefour of France, Wal-Mart of the United States and Sonae of Portugal. Wal-Mart initially adopted a greenfield investment strategy, but in 2004 it acquired the large Brazilian retail chain Bompreço and established itself as the market leader in the north-eastern part of the country. Sonae has acquired medium-sized Brazilian retail chains to ensure growth and market coverage. In Chile the supermarket chains are dominated by the domestic retailers D&S and Jumbo, which have expanded and consolidated at a slower pace than the multinational

Table 1.8   Share of the five largest retailers, selected Latin American countries, 2001–2 (per cent)

	Share of the top five supermarket chains in total supermarket sales	Share of companies with full or partial foreign ownership in top five chains' sales
Argentina	76	84
Brazil	47	91
Chile	55	18
Colombia	72	83
Costa Rica	96	89
Guatemala	99	94
Honduras	71	46
Mexico	80	89

Source: Adapted from Reardon and Berdegué (2002).

retailers that dominate most of the Latin American retail sector. The largest global retail companies operating in Latin America in 2004 are shown in Table 1.9.

Retailing in Latin America has been affected by the economic crises and the consequent reduction of people's disposable income. While the currency devaluation in Brazil in 1998–99 increased consumer confidence and spending, the energy crisis of 2001 and the recession of 2003 had

Table 1.9   Large global retailers with operations in Latin America, 2004

Retailer	Countries	Worldwide sales (US$ billion)
Wal-Mart (United States)	Brazil, Argentina, Mexico	244.5
Carrefour (France)	Brazil, Argentina, Mexico, Chile, Colombia, Dominican Republic	64.7
Ahold (The Netherlands)	Argentina, Brazil, Chile, Costa Rica, Ecuador, El Salvador, Guatemala, Honduras, Nicaragua, Paraguay, Peru	59.2
Costico (United States)	Mexico	38.0
Ito-Yokado (Japan)	Mexico	27.2
Auchan (France)	Argentina, Mexico	25.9
Casino (France)	Argentina, Brazil, Colombia, Mexico	21.5
Delhaize Group (Belgium)	Argentina, Brazil, Colombia, Mexico	19.4

Source: Adapted from www.supermarketnews.com.

a negative impact on spending. In Argentina the debt default from 2001–2 had devastating consequences for retailers as the country experienced high inflation and consumers were impelled to loot supermarkets to obtain food. The performance of the retail sector is closely linked to purchasing power, which has fallen significantly since 2000. While the demand for goods by rural consumers and those on lower incomes has generally grown, the better-off groups have reduced their demand. Moreover the constant economic instability in the region has resulted in high price sensitivity, prompting price wars among retailers, and especially food retailers.

Another major trend in the retail sector is the growth of up-market fashion stores targeting the middle and upper classes. Domestic fashion brands such as Carlota Joakino, Gloria Coelho, Andrea Soletto, Ricardo Almeda and Victor Hugo exist side by side with global brands. Armani, Cartier, Prada and Versace have established premises in a few countries and have been most successful in attracting clientele in Brazil, Argentina, Chile and Mexico. American brands such as Timberland, Tommy Hilfiger and Nautica are sold in all countries but they have limited appeal to most Latin American consumers because they are not well known. The European fashion brands Montblanc, Hugo Boss, Jacadi and L'Occitane have greater appeal and attract sophisticated consumers as European fashion houses are universally acknowledged to be at the cutting edge of design.

The historical connections of Latin Americans with Europe and the significant presence of European businesses in the region play an important part in brand awareness. The principal markets for such brands are the large urban centers where retail outlets pay great attention to shop window display, originality, excitement and service. These shops cater to a rather small segment of consumers who have high requirements in terms of shopping atmosphere and personalized service.

Internet marketing

Marketers are making increasing use of the internet and integrating it into their marketing strategies. The internet has removed the limits on conventional marketing campaigns and changed the nature of product and service distribution.

Regular surveys of the activities of the main Latin American internet service providers (ISPs) show that by the end of 1996 there were more than one million business and individual internet users. Moreover their number was doubling each month. Brazil, Chile and Mexico had the largest ISPs in Latin America. Since its introduction in the early 1990s the internet has penetrated universities, financial services, vehicle dealerships, computer companies and consulting services. The pace of internet growth has exceeded expectations, with more than 100 per cent growth between 1997 and 1999 and over 150 per cent in 2000–3. In most countries the internet is used for educational, business and communication purposes, but in Cuba it is seen as a means to convey political propaganda (Reilly, 1999) and is still a luxury.

Nazco surveys show that more than 90 per cent of internet users in Latin America belong to socioeconomic classes A and B, although the number of class C internet users is rising (www.nua.ie/surveys/index). More than 80 per cent of the websites are in English but the most frequently visited sites are in Spanish and Portuguese. Younger people have taken the lead in internet use, generally in internet rooms and cafés. The establishment of such places has grown at a greater pace than domestic internet connections.

The internet has also aided the internationalization efforts of large Latin American companies, mostly for business-to-business rather than business-to-consumer operations. Small and medium-sized firms are less inclined to use the internet due to the relatively high cost of internet provision and some cultural resistance to it. However the adoption of the internet by Latin American governments has sent a strong message to firms to step up their internet use. It should be mentioned that the informal economy has been shut out of the internet revolution and in many countries – such as Colombia, Peru and Venezuela – the telecommunication infrastructure is so underdeveloped that the majority of the population is shut out of the on-line connectivity.

Online retailing is expanding rapidly in Latin America. In 2002 Brazil had the largest online retail market, with an annual revenue of US$300 million or about half the value of the whole market. Next came Mexico and Argentina, where online retailing generated about US$100 million each. The infrastructure for online retailing is still being developed and has not yet reached the US and West European standard. This is hindering the growth of the sector, as are limited computer ownership and internet access and the low purchasing power of the majority of the population. Urban consumers account for the bulk of online purchases. In rural areas the small percentage of people who have access to the internet continue to trust more in face-to-face buyer–seller relationships.

Three major types of transaction account for about two thirds of the revenue generated by internet sales. The most popular are consumer-to-consumer auctions as they offer bargain prices. Their success is mostly associated with massive marketing campaigns and ease of payment and delivery. Computer hardware, software, video games and supplies account for 15 per cent of online sales. Online financial services are becoming ever more popular in the countries with highest personal computer ownership. A drawback for their growth is that online security cannot be guaranteed on computers in public places such as internet cafés.

The online retail market in Latin America is highly concentrated, and in 2001 the top 20 online retailers accounted for about 75 per cent of the revenue. To become more viable the smaller retailers will have to consolidate and focus on improved customer service, shortened delivery times, competitive pricing policy and a broader selection of products, as well as improving the attractiveness of their websites.

Conclusion

With more than 13 per cent of the world's land mass and about 9 per cent of the population, Latin America accounts for less than 7 per cent of global GDP. In 2001 the region's share in world trade was 12.8 per cent.

The region has undergone turbulent political, economic and social transformation. The recent liberalization of national economies and the privatization of productive assets has improved the business climate and enhanced the trade and investment performance of companies. International trade has intensified, with an increase in both exports and imports. Dynamic capital inflows and outflows have facilitated the internationalization of Latin American firms. The increased FDI inflows have brought competitive pressures that have forced local companies to improve their efficiency and consolidate their operations.

Political and economic reforms have improved most macroeconomic indicators. This has translated into reduced inflation, general stabilization of fiscal and monetary policies, and positive trends in GDP growth. The traditional reliance on the agricultural sector has given way to services and industrial production, which now contribute substantially to employment and GDP.

In comparison with other regions of the world, such as Southeast Asia and Central and Eastern Europe, Latin America has lagged behind in terms of increased gross regional product and, per capita GDP, industrialization and socioeconomic development. The significant size of the informal sector has put tremendous pressure on the formal sector in countries such as Peru and has adversely affected the social welfare system.

The sociodemographic characteristics of the region have been changing since the 1950s, with continuous urbanization and a growing number of dual-income families. However living standards have not improved as the purchasing power of the average household has fallen. Moreover the disparities in income distribution have worsened.

On average consumers have low purchasing power. The total number of people in socioeconomic classes A to C (high to moderate incomes) is about 165 million, while the mass market consists of about 385 million class D and E citizens with extremely low, mostly irregular incomes. Because of this marketers need to find an appropriate marketing strategy based on the product benefit–value–price relationship to target the bottom of the Latin American pyramid. This is especially challenging in Nicaragua, Colombia, Peru and Venezuela, where at least 80 per cent of the population is poor. In addition companies should develop low-cost products for the mass market and reasonably priced high-value products for affluent consumers. Niche marketing based on product differentiation and uniqueness and health and lifestyle benefits can be successful with the most affluent consumers.

The region's abundant natural resources and innovative and creative but underutilized human resources are essential to industrial growth, agricultural intensification and service expansion. Governments should pay more attention to matters such as infrastructural upgrading, technology transfer, encouraging knowledge-intensive businesses, developing business support structures and tourism. Latin American companies should improve their international competitiveness and boost consumer demand by innovating and producing goods with higher value added.

Recommended reading

Books

Bourguignon, F., F. Ferreira and N. Lustig (eds.) (2004) *The Microeconomics of Income Distribution Dynamics in East Asia and Latin America* (Washington, DC: World Bank).

Bulmer-Thomas, V. (ed.) (2001) *Regional Integration in Latin America and the Caribbean: The Political Economy of Open Regionalism* (Institute of Latin American Studies University of London, United Kingdom).

Cypher, J. and J. Dietz (2004) *The Process of Economic Development* (London: Routledge).

D'Andrea, G. and J. Quelch (2001) *Cases in Strategic Marketing Management: Business Strategies in Latin America* (Englewood Cliffs, NJ: Prentice-Hall).

Davila, A. (2001) *Latinos, Inc.: The Marketing and Making of a People* (Los Angeles, CA: University of California Press).

Harrison, L. (2000) *Underdevelopment Is a State of Mind: The Latin American Case* (New York: Madison Books).

Kirby, P. (2003) *Introduction to Latin America: Twenty-First Century Challenges* (London: Sage).

Kotabe, M. and R. Leal (eds.) (2001) *Market Revolution in Latin America: Beyond Mexico* (Oxford: Pergamon Press).

Robles, F., F. Simon and J. Haar (2002) *Winning Strategies for the New Latin Markets* (Englewood Cliffs, NJ: Prentice-Hall).

Schneider, B. (2004) *Business Politics and the State in Twentieth-Century Latin America* (Cambridge: Cambridge University Press).

Weyland, K. (2004) *The Politics of Market Reform in Fragile Democracies: Argentina, Brazil, Peru, and Venezuela* (Princeton, NJ: Princeton University Press).

Journals

Journal of Latin American Studies.
Latin American Business Review.
Latin American Perspectives: A Journal on Capitalism and Socialism.

2
Latin American Consumer Markets and Marketing[1]

Fernando Robles

Introduction

Latin American consumer markets have gone through turbulent times since the early 1990s. Although periods of growth and recession have affected the region in similar ways, their impact has not influenced consumers in the same way or at the same time. In a short period of time the social fabric of Latin America has changed. The region now has a complex, fluid social mixture of rich and poor, old and young, cosmopolitan and traditional. If we add differences in ethnicity, language and climate, Latin America can be viewed as a rich mosaic that produces a variety of consumption behaviors and different ways of adjusting to events that affect the region.

The family remains the focus of consumption, but the situation is changing rapidly. Families are smaller and more urbanized. Presently family members are working more hours but are generating the same income as before, or even less. The average age of the population is rising rapidly, and by 2015 Latin American demographics will resemble those of the developed countries. Inequality of income distribution remains, and the middle class has been losing its share of total national income for a decade or more. In fact the convergence of the middle- and low-income social classes has prompted a debate on the definition of social classes in Latin America. Education, professional status and relationships with others are now better indicators of social class.

In contrast to the market deprivation of the past, economic liberalization has brought more and better consumer choices, especially in urban markets, and consumers are overwhelmed with alternative products.

To cope with their constrained buying power, consumers constantly seek the best value for money. High economic growth in the early 1990s unleashed a wave of consumer optimism in the region, but it did not last long: people's purchasing power peaked in 1996 and suffered a contraction in 1999. After the deep recession of 2000–2 it is now growing again.

Boom and bust cycles in Latin American consumer markets are not new. Older generations can recall similar economic cycles triggered by volatile commodity prices and world recessions. What is new is that the booms and busts of the past decade have taken place in the context of market liberalization and economic reforms that would ostensibly create a thriving middle class and open most of the region's economies to the global market. As the economic reforms have diminished the role of the state, Latin American families have to shoulder a greater share of the cost of basic social services such as health and education.

The fragmentation, specific nature and different dynamics of Latin American markets pose a challenge to all firms. The unsophisticated approaches of the past to entering and servicing the market, based on geography and socioeconomic structures, did not take account of the diversity of the region. Marketing strategies based on the logic of convergence and similar consumer preferences across the region have not produced good results either. Firms that unravel the complexities of the national markets and identify their differences and similarities will prevail.

This chapter navigates the intricacies of Latin American consumer markets. In the first section the size of the market is analyzed and drivers that could affect future buying power are identified. The consumption patterns in Latin America are investigated in the second section, and in the third the impact of these drivers on consumer behavior is explored. The fourth section analyzes various way of segmenting Latin American markets. In the fifth and sixth sections alternative positioning and brand strategies are discussed. An overview of the media and retail sectors in the region is provided in the seventh section. Finally, recommendations for servicing Latin American consumer markets are offered.

The size of the Latin American market

How large is the Latin American market in comparison with other world markets? The Economist Intelligence Unit (EIU, 2000) provides estimates of total private consumption in several world regions and countries that permit comparison. It is estimated that in Latin America private consumption expenditure (PCE) is US$1222 billion, or 25 per cent of the European and 18 per cent of the North American PCE. Thus the

Latin American market is sizable, attractive and important for any company involved in or attempting internationalization.

How large is the Latin American consumer market? What drives the long-term trends of consumer expenditure? A country's PCE measures the final consumption expenditure of households and the private non-profit institutions that serve households in that country. The Strategy Research Corporation (2001) has developed a buying power model that estimates national and household buying power based on aggregate PCE by socioeconomic strata, and on rural and urban distribution. Table 2.1 shows household buying power by country in 2000. As defined by the Strategy Research Corporation, Latin America excludes all non-Spanish and non-Portuguese speaking countries, the Caribbean countries and Cuba, but includes Puerto Rico and the Dominican Republic. Regional consumer buying power grew from US$1033 billion in 1994 to US$1315 billion in 2000.

A full definition of Latin American market potential should include the Latino population of the United States.[2] This population is estimated to be 34 million or about 12.3 per cent of the total US population. According to official figures, in 2000 there were 8.6 million Latino households with a median income of US$26 628 (New Strategist, 2000). However the Strategy Research Corporation (2000) estimates that there were about 10 million Latino households with a mean household annual buying power of US$34 900. A simple calculation based on the latter estimate yields a consumer buying power of US$325 billion in 2000. Thus the Latino market in the United States contributes US$325 billion of market power to the total Latin American consumer market of US$1640 billion. Other reports put the US Latino market power in the range of US$300–US$452 billion (see Stroudsburg, 1999; *Dallas Morning News*, 8 September 2000). Based on these estimates, the extended Latin American buying power may be in the US$1543–US$1767 billion range.

Total consumer buying power is concentrated in the three largest Latin American markets: Brazil, Mexico and Argentina. In 2000 these three countries accounted for 75 per cent of total buying power and 68 per cent of all households in the region. These percentages would drop to 63 per cent and 64 per cent respectively if Latin Americans in the United States were included. Regardless of definition, it is clear that the three largest economies hold at least two thirds of the market power in the region.

The more affluent markets are Argentina, Mexico, Venezuela, Uruguay and Puerto Rico. The average household income in these countries ranges upwards from US$15000. Mexico, Venezuela and to a lesser extent

Table 2.1 Household buying power in Latin America, 2000

	Buying power in 2000 (US$ billion)	Percentage change since 1997	Number of households in 2000 (thousands)	Percentage change since 1997	Household buying power in 2000 (US$)	Percentage change since 1997
Brazil	386.9	−23.0	54188	6.6	7132	−28.0
Mexico	383.1	62.0	18087	5.9	19989	53.0
Argentina	207	−5.0	10009	3.1	20679	−8.0
Venezuela	73.7	63.0	4702	6.6	15679	53.0
Colombia	54.9	−8.0	7490	7.1	7333	14.6
Chile	47.2	−2.0	3982	5.1	11851	−7.0
Peru	41.9	−12.0	5132	3.6	8160	−15.0
Puerto Rico	24.5	−15.0	1271	9.8	19272	−24.0
Guatemala	16.3	14.7	1758	2.5	9309	9.3
Uruguay	15.8	5.0	993	1.2	15949	4.0
Dominican Republic	13.6	28.0	1759	2.0	7755	22.9
El Salvador	11.0	17.0	1591	1.2	6911	16.0
Ecuador	8.8	−28.0	2731	5.7	3229	−32.5
Paraguay	6.8	19.0	1031	3.7	6598	−24.0
Bolivia	6.2	6.0	1268	1.2	4904	3.0
Costa Rica	6.1	11.0	849	3.3	5752	−17.5
Panama	5.7	29.0	714	2.8	8042	23.7
Honduras	3.8	180.0	1210	4.0	3191	88.0
Nicaragua	2.2	29.0	953	3.4	2289	15.0
Total Latin America	1315.5	3.0	120794	5.6	n.a.	n.a.
Latin Americans in the United States	325.0	n.a.	9326	5.6	34900	n.a.
Extended Latin America	1640.5	n.a.	130120	n.a.	n.a.	n.a.

Source: Strategy Research Corporation (2001).

Uruguay experienced income gains between 1997 and 2000, but the other countries suffered a reduction in household income. For example Puerto Rican households lost 24 per cent of their buying power.

In the second group of high- to middle-income countries the average household incomes range from US$7000 to US$15000. In Chile the average annual household buying power is about US$12000. In Brazil,

Colombia, Peru, Panama, Guatemala and the Dominican Republic it ranges from US$7000 to US$10 000. Household buying power in Brazil, Colombia and Peru fell moderately in 1997–2000, while in the smaller economies in this group – Guatemala, Panama and the Dominican Republic – it rose.

In the final group of countries household incomes amount to less than US$8000 per year. This group consists primarily of the Central American countries, Bolivia and Paraguay.

Most Latin American countries experienced sustained growth in consumer buying power in the early 1990s. The exception was Mexico, where consumers lost almost 40 per cent of their buying power in 1995 after the strong devaluation of the peso in December 1994. Latin American consumer buying power started to decline in 1998 after the Brazilian currency reforms, contracted strongly in 1999 and began a gradual recovery in 2000. In the second half of the 1990s Mexico and Venezuela were exceptions to the general decline in consumption power in the region. In the case of Mexico, its integration into the North American Free Trade Agreement (NAFTA) and the favorable oil prices during this period insulated the economy from the regional recession.

In the US Latino population, Cubans are one of the smallest groups but have the highest levels of household income. The median household income for Cuban households in 2000 was estimated at US$44 760. The next group in terms of affluence were Latinos of Central or South American origin, with median incomes of US$39 000, followed by Mexicans (average income of US$32 400) and Puerto Ricans (US$30 300) (Strategy Research Corporation, 2000).

Drivers of buying power in Latin American markets

Many factors influence consumer behavior. The principal ones are economic insecurity, demographic shifts and income distribution. This section provides a brief account of how these drivers affect the buying power of Latin American consumers.

Economic insecurity

Consumption levels in Latin America adjust quickly to external shocks but take a long time to regain past levels. The region's history of repeated booms and busts has had a strong effect on consumer confidence and consumption patterns. Wage earners, who represent the principal market for many consumer items, have experienced a roller coaster of volatility. As macroeconomic and structural reforms worked themselves through the economies of Latin America, labor markets have experienced large fluctuations in employment, unemployment and earnings. Economic insecurity refers to the uncertain environment faced by households and wage earners due to erratic movements in key economic variables such as prices, employment, income and real wages (Lara, 2000). Economic insecurity arises from two sources: external shocks from changes in global financial and product markets, and rapid changes in a given sector due to the obsolescence of skills, radical changes in technology or resource allocation changes across different sectors of the economy.

Annual changes in consumption levels result from the adjustment of consumption to the uncertainty created by these two forces. The variability of such changes over time can be estimated by the extent to which they depart from a long-term average or mean value.[3] A World Bank study of long-term patterns of aggregate private consumption found that in the 1990s volatility in Latin America was three times greater than in the world's advanced economies and above the levels in South Asia and the Middle East. Higher consumption volatility occurred only in Africa, East and Central Asia and the Pacific countries (ECLAC, 2000). According to the World Bank the largest variability in annual consumption growth, defined as variability in excess of 10 per cent, took place in the smaller economies in Latin America, such as Panama, Paraguay and to a lesser extent Chile. It is interesting to note that Chile is by far the most open and liberalized economy in the region, and because of this it is more exposed to external shocks than the other countries in Latin America. As Chilean economic sectors such as mining and agriculture are highly integrated into the world economy they are more likely to be quick to adjust their wage and employment levels to price and demand fluctuations in world markets.

Demographic shifts

Latin American households have become multigenerational units, packed into large urban centers, with two or more income earners, diminishing leisure time and less money dedicated to spending. A major shift in population demographics has driven this change. The shift is characterized by nuclear families of smaller size, an aging population, increased concentration of buying power among urban dwellers, huge social class inequality, and growth in the number of women wage earners and female heads of households.

Because of the baby boom in the 1970s by 2025 the age distribution of the population of Latin America will resemble that in the developed world. The population growth rates in certain countries, for example Argentina, Chile and Uruguay, are rapidly falling. In other countries the developing country profile persists, with high population growth, low life expectancy, high infant mortality and an extremely young population. Based on population growth dynamics the countries can be separated into three groups (*Business Latin America*, 23 June 1997). The countries in the first group – Argentina, Chile, Puerto Rico and Uruguay – now have population growth rates of 1 per cent or less, smaller households of 3.4 members and a rapidly aging population. In the countries of the second group, population growth has fallen to 1–2 per cent and the average household consists of 4.63 members. These countries will reach the 1 per cent population growth rate level in 2020–25. The shift will be more dramatic in Brazil and Mexico, whose populations are currently large and young. The other countries in this group are Colombia, Peru and Ecuador. The third group consists of the rest of the countries in the region, which are characterized by vigorous population growth and an average household size of 5.36 members.

The US Latino population is also young: the median age is 24.8 years, in contrast with the median age of 38.4 years for the rest of the US population. About 36 per cent of Latinos are aged 20 or younger.[4] The average size of Latino households is 3.6 people and the majority of households are located in metropolitan areas. With this profile, the US Latino consumer market resembles that of Puerto Rico.

Smaller household size can restrict household buying power as there are fewer members contributing to the household income. Latin American nuclear families tend to pool their income and share major purchases such as cars and domestic appliances (see Holcombe, 1994, for a discussion of household buying power). The aging of the population will be disadvantageous in countries where the nuclear family is shrinking, and particularly in the case of poor families as one of their ways of coping with declining buying power is to send more members of the family out to work, often adolescents aged 12 and over. In countries where pension systems are in place the pensions received by senior family members contribute only a little to household income: 57 per cent in Uruguay and Argentina, and 2 per cent in Chile and Panama (ECLAC, 2000). Thus multigenerational households will have to adapt their consumption patterns in the future. As the dynamics of economic and social transition work their way through the region the market for services will boom and that for consumer goods will decline.

Increased concentration of buying power in urban centers

About 70 per cent of Latin American buying power is concentrated in 10 metropolitan areas. Here the markets have reached saturation point because of the huge number of incumbent firms and the recent entry of new competitors as a result of market liberalization and deregulation. The second tier of somewhat smaller cities will be the battleground for further growth. Understanding the process of urbanization and the transformation of Latin American cities is essential for market planning.

The relentless process of migration to cities continued unabated in the 1990s, and by 2000 almost 75 per cent of the Latin American population lived in cities (CEPAL, 2000a). There are 52 cities with populations of over one million; 13 in Brazil alone. Eighty per cent or more of the populations of Venezuela, Argentina, Chile and Brazil live in cities. Furthermore trade integration with North America through NAFTA and regional trade integration within MERCOSUR has stimulated labor mobility and the concentration of complementary industrial activities. As a result increased urbanization has occurred along the US–Mexican border and the border between Paraguay and Brazil in the Alto Parana area.

Latin American cities have always been not only magnets for people but also political, economic and cultural centers. The concentration of buying power is quite apparent in the 10 largest markets, which account for 69 per cent of total urban buying power. In 2000 the average household income in the largest urban markets ranged from a low US$8192 in Rio de Janeiro to US$28 210 in Caracas and US$30 959 in Mexico City. If the next 10 largest metropolitan markets are included the concentration of urban buying power rises to a massive 83 per cent.

The US Latino market is also concentrated in a few geographic areas. California, Texas and New York account for 62 per cent of people of Latin American origin or descent living in the United States. Thirty-six per cent of Latino people live in Los Angeles, New York and Miami. According to the Strategy Research Corporation (2000), these three metropolitan areas account for 38 per cent of the US$325 billion market power of Latino consumers in the United States.

Latin American marketers noted the concentration of market power and decided to focus on the large urban markets first. The penetration of certain products is greater than the size of the consumer base, and therefore some urban markets are oversupplied with particular goods. The share of sports shoes in major Latin American cities is 30 per cent, which is in proportion with the share of these cities' inhabitants in the total population. The share of certain brands in urban markets, however, ranges from 17 per cent to 46 per cent, suggesting that the producers of some brands have not made an effort to penetrate secondary cities or rural markets.

As noted earlier, second-tier cities will be the battlegrounds for future growth, and global and national discount and grocery stores are already in the process of entering secondary cities, having spent the last 10 or 15 years building a base in the largest markets. The giant global retailers with a presence in Argentina are now expanding their operations to secondary markets in the interior of the country. After entering Argentina in 1982, Carrefour concentrated on building up its business in greater Buenos Aires. As there was little competition from domestic firms or other global retailers the company had ample time to plan its expansion. However the entry of Wal-Mart in 1994 and the emergence of a strong domestic competitor, Disco, changed the competitive situation. In 1994 self-service stores accounted for 67 per cent of all store space in Buenos Aires but only 45 per cent in the interior. Between 1994 and 1999 the rate of growth of self-service stores in the interior, however, surpassed that in Buenos Aires. In 1999 Wal-Mart entered the coveted Mendoza market. In the same year Disco acquired local food chain stores in Cordoba, San Juan and La Plata and took over the national food chain Ekono. Thus in just one year Disco doubled its number of stores. Retail space in food chains grew at the rate of 26.8 per cent in the interior and 19.5 per cent in Buenos Aires. With this rapid increase and given the small population base, by 1999 these stores controlled 79 per cent of all store space in the interior and 86 per cent in Buenos Aires (Mercardo, 1999).

Dual-income families and female-headed households work

The number of dual-income families in Latin America has been increasing. Female employment has always been common among the poor, but in recent times women from all classes have joined the workforce and contributed to the household income. This is likely to result in postponed or reduced procreation and smaller family size.

Women make up approximately 30 per cent of the workforce in Latin America (Holcombe, 1994). A longitudinal study of urban labor markets in Latin American countries has shown that women's participation in the labor force increased steadily during the 1990s (CEPAL, 2000b). The levels of participation ranged from 44 per cent in Brazil to 38 per cent in Colombia, 34 per cent in Venezuela and 32 per cent in Argentina. While in all countries the percentage of working women had increased at all socioeconomic levels, as could be expected the percentage was higher in low-income parts of the society in all countries. In Colombia, for instance, 56 per cent of women of working age were employed (ibid.). Although in many cases the wages of women are low, they are a welcome addition to household income.

Another example of the changing role of women in Latin America is the rise of female-headed households. Factors affecting this trend include an increase in the divorce rate, the widespread practice of consensual union of cohabitations often headed by women and an increase in the occurrence of widowhood due to political violence and crime. According to one survey, in Argentina, Brazil, Chile, Colombia, Mexico, Peru and Venezuela 24.6 per cent of households are headed by a woman.[5] In Colombia the figure is 31 per cent, possibly due to this country's civil warfare. As could be expected, more households in the lower socioeconomic brackets are female-headed (30 per cent) than in the most affluent bracket (14 per cent). By age, the percentage is higher for those in the 45–54 age group and lowest for those aged 19 and under.

Unequal income distribution

The Latin American middle class has been systematically losing its share of national income over the last decade. A study of long-term trends in income inequality shows that inequality grew throughout the region from 1986 to 1989 and tapered off between 1989 and 1996 (Wodon, 2000). It was once thought that policies designed to stimulate economic growth, such as market openness and macroeconomic stability, would reduce inequality, but this has proved not to be the case. Economic growth has reduced poverty. The poverty level in Latin America dropped to 36 per cent in 1997 from a high of 41 per cent in 1990 but inequality remains the same (CEPAL, 2000c). The drastic reduction of inflation in the region appears to have most benefited the poor. In 1990–96 employment grew faster among the poor and more affluent than among those in the middle-income bracket. In the same period income grew faster only for the more affluent (Klein and Tokman, 2000).

Inequality varies within the region. It is worst in Brazil and Bolivia and relatively smaller in Costa Rica and Uruguay (World Bank, 2000).[6] In the 1990s it increased sharply in El Salvador, Honduras, Nicaragua, Peru and Venezuela, slightly in Brazil, Panama and Uruguay, and remained the same in Mexico, Bolivia, Chile, Colombia and Ecuador (Szekely and Hilgert, 1999).

One clear consequence of the change in income distribution is a shrinking middle class. In Argentina the share fell from 27.3 per cent in 1992 to 21 per cent in 1996. In Venezuela, Peru and Chile the shares fell from 27.3 per cent, 24.8 per cent and 22.6 per cent respectively to 21 per cent, 24 per cent and 18 per cent (EIU, 1999).

The impoverishment of the middle class and the growing affluence of the elite has impelled companies to develop two- or three-tiered marketing strategies, depending on the income elasticity of a consumption category. The impact of price or tax increases on consumption categories can increase or decrease income inequality in the population. In Mexico, increased consumption of leisure activities, private transportation, communications, housing, and education have increased inequality in income distribution. Spending on clothing, cars, energy, tobacco, alcohol, water and pasteurized milk is inequality neutral, whereas expenditure on other food items – such as cereals, fruit, public transport, oil, sugar and flour – tend to reduce inequality. Here the implication is clear: the greater the expenditure on communications, culture and education by certain groups of consumers, the greater the inequality. Thus an unintended consequence of marketing strategies that exclusively target the more affluent segments is that they increase income inequality.

Figure 2.1 illustrates the dynamics of market potential in Latin America. The degree of consumer buying power makes countries more or less attractive. This is indicated by the size of the circle for each country, which is proportional to its buying power. Another feature of the figure is the clustering of countries in terms of their degree of market and demographic transformation. Three clusters can be identified. Argentina, Chile, Puerto Rico and Uruguay form the first cluster (the US Latino market could also be grouped into this cluster). These highly urbanized, demographically advanced countries constitute the second largest market in Latin America. The second group, situated in the center of the matrix, consists of a large number of medium-sized countries and the large Brazilian market. This cluster has the greatest buying power in the region. Its country populations are in full transition and the levels of urbanization range from highly urban to somewhat rural. The last cluster is composed of small countries, most of which are in Central America. Their populations are growing rapidly and are largely rural. Clearly, consumers' needs and expectations are different in each cluster, so in terms of marketing it is unlikely that one strategy will appeal to consumers in all clusters.

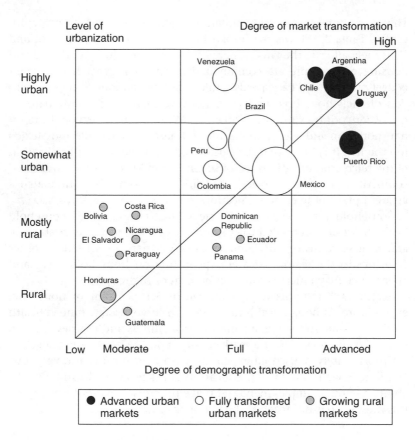

Figure 2.1   Latin American market clusters
Source: Robles *et al.* (2003).

Latin American consumption patterns

With about a third of household budgets being spent on food, the key
to reaching Latin American consumers is through their stomachs. Diets
differ widely and reflect the rich mix of indigenous people and those of
European, African and Asian descent. Although there are substantial
differences among adult consumers, Latin American children have
remarkably similar preferences as they have been raised during a period
of market liberalization and the impact of globalization has tended to
unify consumption patterns.

In general Latin American consumption patterns are typical of countries in the process of economic development and social change.

The consumption patterns of urban and rural consumers differ significantly. Table 2.2 shows that urban households in Argentina, Peru and
Venezuela allocate the largest share of their budgets to food, if food and
housing expenditure are combined they spend at least half of their
budget on these two basic needs. Chilean families allocate a larger proportion of their household budget to housing than their counterparts in
the other countries listed in Table 2.2. With regard to expenditure on
transportation and telecommunications, households in Chile and Mexico
top the list. It is likely that the earlier and more extensive liberalization
of the telecommunications sector in Chile and Mexico – with increased
competition leading to lower prices and more options – stimulated a
greater uptake of telecommunications services in these countries.

Household furnishings are the next largest category of household
expenditure. Households in Peru and Mexico spend more in absolute
and relative terms on this product category than households in other
countries in the region. Greater expenditure on household décor and
appearance may reflect cultural differences or higher prices.

Health care accounts for an average of 5.1 per cent of household
expenditure. Although health care is vital to survival, state funded health
services are rare in the region, and therefore illness and injuries often go
untreated and do not have a marked impact on the household budget.

Unfortunately household expenditure on education is also very low.
While it is well known that education is a key factor in individuals'
ability to obtain employment and make progress in society, apparently
this message has not reached the majority of households.

Table 2.2 Urban household expenditure, selected Latin American countries,
2000 (per cent)

	Argentina	Brazil	Chile	Mexico	Peru	Uruguay	Venezuela	Average
Food	41	30	38	35	43	32	40	37.0
Housing	11	11	14	12	7	12	11	11.2
Transportation and telecommunications	10	11	16	14	7	10	7	10.8
Clothing	9	9	8	7	9	7	7	8.0
Household furnishing	7	7	9	10	11	6	4	7.8
Education and leisure	5	5	8	8	8	4	5	5.9
Health	6	6	4	4	7	6	3	5.1
Other	11	21	3	10	8	23	23	14.2

Source: Strategy Research Corporation (2001).

In summary the analysis of the budget allocations of Latin American households shows a pattern that is typical of developing countries. Only Puerto Rico and to a lesser extent Brazil depart from this profile. In the case of Puerto Rico, the influence of the US consumer culture and prices has resulted in a consumption pattern that is similar to that in the United States.

Consumption of some product categories is sometimes similar and sometimes different across the region. Factors such as income and relative prices have a generalized impact, although consumers in more affluent countries can afford more luxurious and pricier products. Other factors, including culture, climate, local food supplies and degree of urbanization, also determine preferences for certain types of product.

Given that food accounts for a substantial proportion of household expenditure in Latin America we shall look in greater detail at the food consumption patterns in the large and medium-sized countries. In Latin America the rich heritage of indigenous, European and other traditions combine with the diverse climatic and geographic conditions to produce a large variety of food consumption styles. Modernization and globalization have also had an impact on food consumption, for example in terms of there being less time to spend on traditional home cooking. Table 2.3 shows the per capita consumption of several food categories. The United States is included for the purpose of comparison.

Argentineans are the largest consumers of dairy products and meat, which is hardly surprising given that the rich and flat land is ideal for cattle farming. Argentina, Chile and Venezuela are part of the pasta culture, with consumption levels that are 2.6 times higher than in Mexico and Colombia. When it comes to breakfast cereals, Mexico is the only

Table 2.3 Per capita food consumption, selected categories and countries, Latin America, 2000

	Dairy (kg)	Meat (kg)	Pasta (kg)	Breakfast cereal (kg)	Frozen food (kg)	Beverages (liters)	Snacks (kg)
Argentina	228.5	72.3	8.3	0.3	0.6	101.1	4.1
Brazil	61.9	60.0	5.6	1.0	3.9	119.5	6.8
Chile	44.6	62.0	8.7	0.3	2.3	84.1	5.5
Colombia	54.7	34.0	3.1	0.3	1.3	103.8	2.5
Mexico	61.9	49.5	3.1	4.8	2.9	143.9	3.2
Venezuela	10.4	41.7	11.7	0.8	2.8	96.1	5.3
USA	94.5	88.2	3.1	4.5	9.2	321.9	23.7

Source: Euromonitor (1999–2000).

country with a high intake – higher even than in the United States. Proximity to the United States might partly explain this, but it is also likely that employment in the US industrial complexes in Mexico has altered the traditional meal times and necessitated a larger intake of quickly prepared food at breakfast time. The impact of modernization is also apparent in the relatively high consumption of frozen food in Brazil, Mexico and Venezuela. Although the consumption of frozen food is still below the US level it is rising rapidly, with a growth rate of 206 per cent in Brazil and 265 per cent in Colombia in 1993–96 (Euromonitor, 1999–2000).

In contrast to the differences noted above, Latin Americans are very similar when it comes to the consumption of non-alcoholic beverages. Mexicans have the largest per capita consumption, with an intake of 144 liters. Another similarity is that Latin Americans are not large consumers of snacks, whether salty or sweet. However with urbanization, the growth of two-income households, and increased commuting time because of the poor public transport systems in most large Latin American cities, snack consumption is rising. Another factor in this is the growing presence of discount retailers, convenience stores and supermarkets. Manufacturers such as Frito-Lay and Nabisco have reported record sales growth in Latin America.

Some of the differences in food consumption become blurred when one looks at food preferences by age and social class. A study of the food consumed by Latin American children aged seven to 11 found similar consumption patterns across the region. The five most popular food items were rice, chicken, bread, potatoes and eggs, while consumption of vegetables, beans and corn was low (Audit and Surveys Worldwide, 1998). Consumption differences by social class will be examined later.

In summary when it comes to food, Latin America is hardly homogeneous. A variety of food consumption patterns have emerged for different reasons, and food marketers have learned to make adaptations.

The Latin American consumer

Coping with economic cycles

As mentioned earlier, lower inflation and economic growth in the early 1990s brought to the market first-time buyers of a range of consumer durables, and many Latin American people bought their first car, refrigerator or washing machine. Business journals and periodicals were quick to point out this trend, with headlines such as 'Latin America: the big move to free markets' (*Business Week*, 15 June 1992). In Mexico the boom did not last long. As *The Wall Street Journal* put it, 'Peso crisis threatens the Mexican Dream' (*Wall Street Journal*, 11 January 1995). Other Latin American markets weathered the Mexican crisis and continued or began to enjoy market growth. On 9 February 1998 *Business Week* reported that millions of young consumers in Latin America were on a shopping spree and the multinationals raced to attract their attention.

If during times of economic growth everyone wins, when economies contract not everyone loses and countries do not adjust to economic downturns in the same way. Although economic crises are not new to Latin America, previous crises had longer cycles and adjustments, and consumers gradually lost their buying power over a long period. In the 1980s there was a long-term deterioration of living standards throughout the region. The crisis of the 1990s was different. One major difference was that the recession occurred in the context of new market economies. Interest rates for consumer credit increased, and in Brazil the rate doubled to 43 per cent in 1999 (Holcombe, 2000).[7] Older generations of Latin Americans were unable to apply past experience to the new context, and for younger generations the crisis was their first.

To cope with the recession consumers used some strategies that were similar throughout the region and others that were unique to their situation. The common strategies were as follows.

First, they avoided or postponed long-term financial obligations. Many people cancelled their plans to buy cars, household appliances and non-essentials such as family vacations. Second, they renegotiated or cancelled their credit arrangements. Consumers who were unable to meet the high payments for household goods or cars bought on credit returned the goods or declared themselves insolvent. Whether initiated by the borrower or the lender, the holding of credit cards also declined in 1999.

Third, changes were made to the consumption basket. In most countries, expenditure on basic commodities increased, while changes in the consumption of other items varied according to country and culture. An analysis of changes in sales volumes in 1998–9 in Argentina, Brazil and Chile reveals similarities in the purchase of the top main product categories and large differences in others. The largest increases were related to health: infant formulas in Argentina, mineral water in Brazil and pure fruit juices in Chile. Another item whose sales volume increased consistently in all countries was hair colorant. According to local market observers, in the midst of bad times Argentineans wanted to look good and indulge themselves (*Mercado*, November 2000). The largest declines in sales were different in each country. In Brazil the largest decline was in shaving kits. In Argentina it was cookies and in Chile it was insecticide.

Fourth, consumers began to shop in self-service stores, discount stores and large hypermarkets. The entry of foreign discount retailers to the region and the switch by local retailers to the discount format introduced consumers to the concept of own brands and generic products. All of a sudden they had greater product choice and a range of price–quality options. Inevitably this retail segment quickly acquired a substantial market share.[8]

Fifth, consumers searched for a better quality–price ratio. Whereas in the past they had been attracted to low-price products, during crisis it appears that they no longer wished to sacrifice quality. A study of attitudes toward shopping in Colombia revealed that the majority of consumers were opposed to buying unknown brands just to save money. Nonetheless only one in four remained loyal to particular brands. The rest actively sought alternative brands and looked for promotions and special offers (Soong, 2000a). In Argentina in 1999, 25 per cent of consumers were not interested in buying unknown brands to save money (Soong, 2000b). The proportion of consumers who preferred only branded products declined from 46 per cent in 1998 to 22 per cent in 2000. Self-service grocery stores and discount retailers such as Carrefour and Disco seized this opportunity and filled their shelves with their own brands, which were attractively packaged and on average priced 30–40 per cent lower than the premium brands. The sale of good-quality domestic brands also increased. An additional attraction of shopping in discount stores was access to store credit, which seemed to be replacing bank credit.

In summary, in a very short period of time Latin American consumers drastically changed their consumption and shopping habits. The most notable trend was the search for value for money, with consumers constantly evaluating price–quality options.

Searching for value in uncertain times

Consumers in Latin America are constantly developing strategies to cope with money and time limitations. To understand the emergence of new consumer values the principal contributory key factors are explored below.

Realism and cynicism

Latin American consumers are increasingly translating their sensitivity to social issues into consumption decisions. Increasingly visible corruption has resulted in consumer cynicism, especially among younger people.

In the process nostalgic interest in the past and in local identity has emerged. In general consumers have become skeptical of marketing claims, global brands have lost their allure and have a harder time connecting with more disenfranchised market segments, and consumers rely more on retailers for information on products.

The price imperative

Low prices are essential to remaining competitive. Prices have been falling across the region for several years since the peak in 1998 (*The Economist*, 8 September 2001). In most countries, single-digit inflation has been the norm for several years.[9] As the prices of all competing brands have come down, price has ceased to be a differentiating factor and firms have had to decide whether it is better to discount a premium brand or introduce reformulated or new products at lower prices.

Selectivity

As discussed earlier, Latin American consumers are reallocating their shrinking consumption budgets. Non-essential purchases are now postponed and essential goods are prioritized. For example the sale of cars has fallen by 40 per cent in Argentina but refrigerator sales have risen; the consumption of basic personal care products such as toothpaste and deodorants is down but the consumption of all-purpose cleaning products is up. The implication for firms is that consumer selectivity is creating marketing opportunities for some and shrinking the markets for others.[10]

Stretching the budget

An important requirement for Latin American consumers in uncertain times is getting the most from their limited resources. For example buying multipurpose cleaning products in a large economy size is one way of stretching the budget, as is shopping at hard-discount stores. Time is also scarce because of increased work commitments. The growing popularity of food marts in gas stations is one example of how consumers respond to this pressure on their time. Convenience stores offer basic necessities and a range of goods and services such as prepared foods, ATMs and internet kiosks.

Increased awareness of health and the environment

A shift to more healthy diets and concern for the environment are global trends but they intensified in Latin America with the economic crisis. The main driver of better diets is the rise in the cost of health care that has resulted from the reduction of public health-care services. The shift to healthier eating habits is not restricted to more affluent people but is shared by all socioeconomic classes. The demand for healthier products is on the increase. For example consumption of bottled mineral water is up and that of carbonated soft drinks is down, despite price reductions. As large companies are being slow to react to this trend there are opportunities for small national and regional specialists to benefit from entering these market niches.

Self-indulgence

Self-indulgence is one way in which Latin American consumers make themselves feel good in the midst of economic malaise. As the economic crisis has deepened the type and value of the products chosen has varied. In the early part of the recession in Argentina the demand for beauty products remained strong, but as the crisis deepened it shrank while the demand for confectionary increased. Beer sales also remained strong (*Mercado*, 2001).

Consumer values

Four consumer values have emerged Latin America. The first is *economic value*, with consumers searching for multipurpose solutions, convenience and functionality within their budgets. The second, *self-gratification*, is to do with feeling good in the midst of pessimism. However because of their growing concern with their personal health they are turning to simple, immediate and more realistic gratifications.

The third value is a *sense of belonging*. Consumers are returning to local values and icons and look to the past for nostalgic inspiration.

Finally, as part of the general shift towards greater transparency in society, consumers are demanding *honesty and transparency* in commercial activities. Any claim that seems exaggerated erodes consumers' trust.

Marketing strategies have taken account of these values, and any strategy that focuses on just one of them, such as price, is doomed to fail. The final mix will depend on the culture and degree of demographic transformation of the country in question. Some of the values may be more important in some countries and less in others. In Brazil the sense of belonging is an intrinsic part of the national culture. Thus key elements of all marketing strategies in Brazil should be customer service and personalization. In Argentina, given that the deep economic recession has made economic value an overriding factor, an effective strategy would be to economize on customer service and pass on the savings to the customer. Mexican consumers place a high value on shopping time, given Mexico's robust economy until recently. Therefore marketing strategies should stress the value of one-stop shopping, whether for financial services or groceries.

A holistic approach to consumer values, such as one-stop shopping, reasonable credit access, reasonable prices and acceptable quality seems to be the right marketing mix for Latin America. The challenge for premium brands is to justify their position or reduce the price gap between them and shops' own or so-called B brands. Coca-Cola is among the brands that have felt the brunt of alternative offerings in the region. More than 200 soft-drink brands are competing for the US$3.1 billion Argentine market, with B brands accounting for almost a quarter of that market. Whilst Coca-Cola sells for US$1 per 1.5 liters, medium-price brands sell for US$0.64–0.75. Low-price brands, which contain little more than water, artificial colorants and sugar, sell for less than US$0.60 per two liter bottle. When Coca-Cola introduced a fruit-based clear cola named Tai in Brazil and Argentina to challenge the low-priced brands it set an introductory price of US$0.75, but quickly had to lower it to US$0.48 in order to compete. Tai has secured just 0.4 per cent of the market. Meanwhile a Peruvian cola is threatening the dominant position of Coca-Cola and Pepsi in Mexico, Peru and Venezuela. With a very simple approach to distribution and low prices, Kola Real has become a real threat to the two cola powerhouses (*Wall Street Journal Americas*, 27 October 2003) and taken 19 per cent of the market in Peru, 14 per cent in Venezuela and 4 per cent in Mexico. The latter is the second largest cola market in the world after the United States.

Another example of an attempt to address the appreciation of value for money in Latin America is provided by the French chain Carrefour. This retail giant decided to fight against the low-priced brands by introducing its own low-price range, *Sí*, which includes about 500 products. The prices are 30 per cent lower than those of Carrefour's own brand and 40 per cent lower than those of the premium brands. Meanwhile Unilever has successfully defended its brand positioning in Argentina against low-priced detergents by introducing a number of brands aimed at different market segments. Argentine consumers are said to be worried about the performance of low-priced detergents and fear that they might ruin their garments. As noted earlier, Argentineans place great store on personal appearance (ibid.).

Segmenting the Latin American market

Consumer markets are a reflection of society. Latin American society is complex and fragmented, so for marketers market segmentation is required. For many years marketers have segmented the Latin American markets by socioeconomic class and formulated their marketing strategies accordingly. However with fluctuating incomes this strategy is no longer effective and alternative approaches are necessary.

The conventional approach: socioeconomic segmentation

In more advanced countries where reliable household and personal income data are available, segmenting the market by income is practical, but in emerging markets such as the Latin American a classification based purely on income produces suspect results (Walker, 1995). Thus national organizations and marketing institutions use additional measures of social class, such as the educational level of the head of household, occupation, possession of certain household goods, and housing characteristics. Points are allocated for each of these variables and households are classified according to their total points. By this means the Gallup organization categorizes people into five classes: upper class, emerging elite, middle class, working class, and extremely poor (Molina, 1999). The Strategy Research Corporation uses other classifications: upper class (class A), upper-middle class (B), middle-class (C), and low-income or poor (D and E classes). As different national organizations in Latin America use different scoring systems and weights to define basically the same segments, comparing data across countries is rather difficult. However other organizations, including Gallup and Roper Starch, use common definitions when conducting pan-regional surveys.

On average 2.3 per cent of Latin American households are upper class, ranging from a low of 0.9 per cent in Nicaragua to a high of 7.2 per cent in Uruguay. Despite this small percentage, because of the highly unequal income distribution in the region buying power is concentrated in classes A and B, making these segments very attractive to marketers of top of the range products. The largest concentration of buying power in urban markets is found in Venezuela, where just 5.3 per cent of urban households are upper or upper-middle class but they account for 40 per cent of the total urban buying power (Table 2.4). In Brazil 18.6 per cent of urban families in classes A and B account for 63 per cent of urban buying power.

The middle class includes small-business owners, skilled workers and clerical workers with at least primary school education. Incomes fluctuate widely in this segment in accordance with booms and busts in the economy. Chile is the only country with a relatively large number of households in the middle class, which also accounts for a large percentage of buying power. In Latin America as a whole the middle class's share of

Table 2.4 Total buying power in urban areas, by socioeconomic class, selected Latin American countries, 2000

	Urban households (millions)	Urban buying power (US$ billion)	Socioeconomic class			
			Upper class	Upper-middle class	Middle class	Low-income/poor
Argentina	8.9	186.3				
Average household buying power			166 721	54 651	16 940	13 596.0
Percentage of households			1.6	8.3	35.4	54.7
Percentage of buying power			13.0	22.0	29.0	36.0
Brazil	43.3	354.7				
Average household buying power			78 731	15 156	6 392	1 549
Percentage of households			2.6	16.0	28.9	52.5
Percentage of buying power			29.0	34.0	26.0	11.0
Chile	3.4	41.5				
Average household buying power			118 510	43 963	12 475	2 850
Percentage of households			2.1	6.2	41.8	49.9
Percentage of buying power			19.0	23.0	46.0	12.0
Colombia	5.6	47.7				
Average household buying power			79 993	31 711	6 505	1 345
Percentage of households			2.2	7.7	37.1	53.0
Percentage of buying power			24.0	32.0	34.0	10.0
Mexico	14.4	313.9				
Average household buying power			249 201	62 352	25 165	5 856
Percentage of households			1.5	10.9	22.4	65.2
Percentage of buying power			19.0	33.0	29.0	19.0

Table 2.4 (Continued)

	Urban households (millions)	Urban buying power (US$ billion)	Socioeconomic class			
			Upper class	Upper-middle class	Middle class	Low-income/poor
Peru	3.7	37.1				
Average household buying power			78 989	33 623	8 309	1 186
Percentage of households			2.5	8.2	32.9	56.4
Percentage of buying power			23.0	35.0	34.0	8.0
Venezuela	4.1	68.7				
Average household buying power			216 661	94 077	33 231	3 573
Percentage of households			1.1	4.2	20.1	74.6
Percentage of buying power			15.0	25.0	43.0	17.0
Latin America	93.2	730.0				
Average household buying power			91 450	31 591	10 347	3 168
Percentage of households			2.2	12.4	29.6	55.8
Percentage of buying power			19.6	26.0	37.8	16.5

Source: Strategy Research Corporation (2001).

buying power has declined or stagnated in recent years as a result of economic crises and other factors. For example an analysis of the impact of Mexican peso devaluation conducted by the Strategy Research Corporation showed that the percentage of households classified as middle class fell from 58 per cent in 1994 to 36.9 per cent in 1996. By 2000 the figure had fallen to just 22.4 per cent. Thus many middle-class families moved down the income ladder in 1994–2000.

Upper-class Mexican households have the highest incomes in Latin America, followed closely by their Venezuelan counterparts. Households in these two countries have over 2.5 times the average income of Latin American households in this class. Table 2.4 shows the perils of classifying households in class segments based on income alone. If income were the only indicator, Argentine poor households would be classified as middle class in all Latin American countries but Mexico and Venezuela.

Other segmentation approaches

Greater ownership of household goods such as color TV and telephones across socioeconomic segments is blurring the distinction between classes, despite income differences. Thus other segmentation approaches have been developed to address these differences. The J. W. Thompson group uses two simple indicators – education and profession – to define social class. Under this classification the upper class consists of college-graduate owners and top executives of large firms. The upper-middle class is composed of executives and owners of firms who have had some college education but do not hold a college degree. In the middle class are middle-level professionals, employees, public servants, skilled workers and small business owners. The people in this group have either a high school diploma or a vocational certificate. The next group is made up of unskilled workers and new entrants to the labor market with primary school education. The lowest level consists of individuals without permanent employment and little or no primary education.

Based on this classification, J. W. Thompson states that 4 per cent of Chilean society can be classified as upper class, 10 per cent as upper-middle class, 38 per cent as middle class, 38 per cent as lower class and 10 per cent as poor (*La Tercera*, 9 September 1999). Interestingly, under the new definition the upper class is twice as large as it is using the conventional classification, in combination the size of the upper and upper-middle class is larger and more in line with the average for the region, and the size of the middle class is lower and in line with those in other Latin American countries. In other words, judged on income alone the middle class is overestimated when the conventional classification is used.

Thus J. W. Thompson's definition may provide a better indication of likely consumption patterns and is therefore more useful for the formulation of marketing strategies.

Another market segmentation approach is to group consumers into lifestyle segments according to their activities, interests and opinions. Audits and Surveys Worldwide (1996) conducted a study of Latin American consumers and identified five distinct groups. The first group, labeled image seekers, was composed of teenagers who lived at home, were up to date with styles and fashions, and were willing to try new things. The second group, 'curious cosmopolitans', were college students with a variety of interests and keen to visit new places and learn about other cultures. The third group, labeled global professionals, consisted of affluent, college-educated males aged 18–34 from socioeconomic class A or B who were willing to pay for high-quality brands. The fourth group, 'concerned traditionalists', were aged 35–54, married with children, concerned about the cost of products, worried about job loss, cared for the environment, preferred domestic products and avoided up-to-date technology. Those in the final group were aged 50 or over, married with children, of lower socioeconomic class, preferred to watch TV and were not interested in new things. As can be seen, classification according to lifestyle also reveals that individuals' consumption patterns and needs change with age.

The Brazilian firm IBOPE (2000) has used this approach and seven life stages to segment the large Brazilian market. The percentage of Brazilian households in each stage from youth to empty nest and the changes in their relative share over a six-year period were evaluated. The analysis revealed significant differences in consumption levels between groups across a range of consumer categories, including beverages, milk, snacks, and toothpaste.

Similarly Arellano (2000) has used nine lifestyle segments in a study of Peru. The segments and their share of the Peruvian population were as follows: economizers (20.5 per cent), traditionalists (18.1 per cent), progressives (17.6 per cent), survivors (16.0 per cent), adapters (8.2 per cent), workers (10.5 per cent), fortunates (4.2 per cent), entrepreneurs (2.8 per cent) and hedonists (2.1 per cent). According to Arellano each of the groups has its own strategy for coping with the volatility and economic hardships that Peruvian society has experienced in recent decades. Moreover its members come from all socioeconomic classes. For instance 'progressives' (characterized by a motivation to achieve, a strong work ethic and emphasis on education) come from the upper class (4.9 per cent), middle class (11.8 per cent), lower class (40.7 per cent) and the poor (42.6 per cent).

Segmentation of the Latino population in the United States is based on descriptors such as generation, degree of acculturation and country of origin. The generational groups are divided into those born in the United States and those born in Latin America. According to the Strategy Research Corporation (2000), 72 per cent of Latinos living in the United States in 2000 were born in Latin America, 14 per cent were first-generation Americans, 5 per cent were second generation and 9 per cent were third generation. The main consumption difference between US-born Latinos and Latinos who had emigrated to the United States was in the possession of cellular phones and personal computers with internet access. In this regard the US born Latino was the same as the non-Latino population, whereas the possession level among those who had emigrated was much lower.

Degree of acculturation refers to the extent to which Latinos view themselves as part of the mainstream US culture. Acculturation can be measured by a number of indicators, such as the language used for daily exchanges and the number of years of education received in the United States. In 2000 11 per cent of US Latinos were highly acculturated, 64 per cent were partly acculturated and 25 per cent were not acculturated (ibid.) Analysis of personal possessions by degree of acculturation revealed significant differences between the unacculturated group and the other two. The acculturated groups had greater ownership of products such as automobiles, cable television, cellular phones and credit cards, with levels close to the US average. Finally, by country of origin, Latinos of Mexican background account for 63.3 per cent, Central and South Americans for 15 per cent, Puerto Ricans for 10.5 per cent and Cubans for about 5 per cent.

Summary

The above discussion has shown that there are many ways to identify market segments, and that the use of socioeconomic class as the sole basis for segmentation does not provide a full picture of the Latin American market reality. A better solution is to combine several approaches and identify the one combination that corresponds best to the type of business or consumer category one is analyzing, for example a combination of lifestyle segments and socioeconomic class. Market success may depend on seeing opportunities for positioning and segmentation where others see only threats.

A complication arises with pan-regional analyses. Life-cycle segments can be found in any country. The proportion and characteristics may vary but the definition of the segments is invariable. On the other hand lifestyle segments may be nation specific and unique to each country and market culture. For example in Peru particular lifestyles may be associated with coping with a harsh and volatile macroeconomic environment that does not exist elsewhere.

One means of simplifying the complexity of segments and market contexts in Latin America is to use a nesting approach that moves from the general to the specific. For instance, at the first level of analysis a socioeconomic approach can be used to determine strategies for the socioeconomic classes. At the second level, strategies can be based on life-cycle segments. At the third level, lifestyles are investigated to determine the market positioning of firms and their offering for one or several segments in a given country.

Positioning strategies for Latin American markets

The conventional approach

A dramatic realignment of consumers' expectations has challenged the conventional positioning strategy based on socioeconomic segmentation. With this it is assumed that product markets first develop in affluent segments and then trickle down to the masses over time. Both products and strategies are differentiated for the various segments. Take for instance Whirlpool's approach to marketing refrigerators and washing machines in Argentina. The firm targets products bearing its Whirlpool brand name at the more affluent families in the ABC1 socioeconomic classes and its basic and affordable Eslabón de Lujo brand targets the C2 and C3 socioeconomic segments.[11] Both brands are manufactured in Argentina. The company has plans to segment the market even further and introduce a low-price, kerosene-powered refrigerator for rural households with no electricity supply (*Meio & Messagem*, 14 March 2001, 7 May 2001).

The conventional approach worked well when the socioeconomic boundaries were stable and market competition was mainly among domestic firms, but as discussed earlier economic volatility and financial hardship have resulted in a blurring of the socioeconomic class distinctions. Another factor that has challenged the conventional approach is the skepticism about premium brand products. As consumers' expectations have become more realistic they constantly evaluate the price to value ratio of alternative product choices. There is evidence that younger consumers in Latin America are more pragmatic, less committed and distrustful of the claims made for products. Moreover domestic competitors are closing the quality gap between their products and global brands, and discount stores and supermarkets have been very successful in marketing their own-label brands at substantially lower prices than those of premium brands.

An emerging approach: convergence towards the center

Two new marketing strategies appear to be promising in respect of delivering consumer value. The goal of the first strategy is to attract affluent consumers (ABC1) who are under economic pressure, consumers from the embattled middle class (C2 and C3) and consumers in the popular segment (D) by offering the best possible value for money. A key element of this strategy is integrating all the dimensions of consumer value discussed above under a single brand offering. In essence the firm becomes an integrator of services and aggregator of market segments, and it aspires to offer world-class quality in the local market.[12]

The second strategy is aimed at the top end of the market and commodities the notion of premium. As products are easily imitated, many companies are differentiating their products from those of their competitors by providing value-added personal services. These operations are often spin-offs from mainstream operations and the products are given another brand name. For example Banco Itau's Personnalité business offers personalized service, financial advice and special investment products in a network of special branches in Brazil. Since the introduction of Personnalité in 1999, Itau has attracted 12000 new customers.[13]

New market entrants are also changing the definition of premium products and services. For instance France's Louis Vuitton Moet Hennessy (LVMH) has redefined the meaning of up-market in respect of accessories, clothing and cosmetics. In 1999 LVMH opened its first Latin American retail store in São Paulo, where it offered an assortment of luxury leather goods, champagne and cognac, perfumes, cosmetics, watches and jewelry with top brand names such as Dom Perignon, Hennessy, Louis Vuitton and Christian Dior. Following the success of this store LVMH opened a second one in São Paulo and others in Rio de Janeiro, Brasília and Mexico City. Other up-market retailers, including Tiffany, have adopted a similar approach.

Specialists can also be found at the lower end of the market. Here the strategy is to combine convenience with low prices in order to build up demand rapidly and provide the wherewithal for expansion. For example chains of small self-service pharmacies that cater to the mass market are now competing successfully with large discount and supermarket chains by combining low prices with convenient location. Further examples of specialist strategies will be provided in the section on retailing.

Brand strategies in volatile and uncertain markets

Building up a strong brand, whether global or domestic, is the prime goal of any business strategy. The challenge is to build one that resonates with the market reality.

The power of global and domestic brands

Global brands entering Latin American markets capitalize on their world-class status and technological superiority, and appeal to consumers' aspiration for a cosmopolitan and sophisticated lifestyle. Multinational companies have invested substantial amounts in promoting their brands in Latin America and tend to enjoy a consistent market positioning.

Familiarity is important to consumers who are reluctant to experiment with new products or ideas and are not interested in global culture. Domestic brands derive their market power from their identification with local values, folklore and traditions. Since they have been conceived and produced for the local market, consumers perceive them as more suited to their lives and circumstances. Domestic brands have improved considerably in terms of quality and performance, and a number of companies have reengineered their production processes to become more cost efficient.

Past brand-building efforts and investments have paid off well for both global and domestic brands, and the most successful have gained admiration and respect among Latin American consumers.

One way of determining the impact of brand building is by assessing brand equity. With this approach a brand is financially evaluated to assess its likely contribution to future revenues and the profitability of the firm. Although global brands have been regularly valued for investment and other purposes, until recently Latin American brands have not been similarly evaluated. The first such exercise was conducted by the consultancy firm Interbrand, which found that the Brazilian brands with the highest equity (financial valuation) were Banco Itau, Bradesco, AmBev (Brahma-Antarctica), Banco do Brasil, Unibanco, Embraer (a commuter aircraft manufacturer), Multibras, Embratel, Gradiente (electronics), Sadia and Tigre. With a brand equity of US$970 million, Banco Itau ranked seventy-fifth on the list of the top 100 global brands (*Meio & Messagem*, 14 March 2001).

Brand erosion and migration to the middle ground

Brand equity is difficult to sustain during times of economic hardship. As discussed earlier, Latin American consumers seek value for money, self-gratification, transparency and a sense of community. Brands that are out of touch with this reality become irrelevant. Stores' own-label and discount brands have struck a chord with Latin American consumers. According to ACNielsen (2000) the proportion of consumers who bought own-label brands rose in Argentina, from 44 per cent in 1998 to 60 per cent in 2000. In the latter year the sales volume of non-branded products increased by 2 per cent and that of branded products fell by 6.6 per cent.

When global brands enter a local market they have a premium positioning and appeal mostly to class A and B consumers with internationalizing lifestyles or aspirations. More often than not, competing domestic brands are positioned at the lower end of the price and quality ladder. In order to close the gap domestic producers take steps to improve the quality of their products, with a consequent price increase. Meanwhile the price of leading brands is reduced to make them more affordable. As the price gap diminishes the market becomes commoditized, necessitating brand revitalization by means of innovation and differentiation. In most cases this is incremental in nature and easily imitated by domestic companies and retailers, so the cycle of commoditization begins anew.

The economic situation in Latin America has changed this traditional process in two ways. First, because of financial pressure some Latin American consumers have stoped buying certain products altogether and restricted their expenditure to essentials. Once this has happened the trend is difficult to reverse. Second, if a brand is out of touch with the economic reality, any effort to revitalize it will be wasted.

To break the brand erosion cycle in Latin America, firms should adopt a systematic brand building strategy that will ensure market relevance, deliver consumer value and eliminate consumer confusion.

Building brand equity in uncertain times

A systematic brand strategy is a carefully orchestrated effort to develop a brand architecture to support the goal of establishing value, relevance and resonance. This architecture consists of several building blocks (Keller, 1997; Aaker and Joachimsthaler, 2000).

The first building block consists of advertising to establish brand salience. Unsurprisingly the top advertisers in Latin America are large multinational companies with a broad portfolio of brands, such as

Nestlé, Unilever, Procter & Gamble, Colgate Palmolive and Coca-Cola. Among the few domestic companies and brands that are heavy investors in advertising are Banco Itau (Brazil), Quilmes (Argentina), Telmex (Mexico), Polar beer (Venezuela), and Cristal beer (Peru).

The second building block is brand meaning and the goal is to establish credibility. This involves conveying value for money and brand personality. With the latter the aim is to bring out aspects of history, heritage and experience that can make the brand relevant to Latin American consumers. In times of financial crisis Latin Americans tend to favor familiar icons and local heritage, hence giving an advantage to domestic brands.

The third building block is emotional response. Here the firm seeks positive responses to and judgments of the brand and the firm that go beyond product or service performance. The aim is to assure consumers of the brand's achievements over time and commitment to the future. The strategy links the brand to corporate competence, innovativeness and trustworthiness. Take for instance the case of Telefónica Spain. When the firm took over the privatized public telephone networks in many Latin American countries its goal was to provide a basic service to as many people as possible. During the network building and improvement phases the Telefónica brand stood for fulfilment of the promise to install telephones. When the monopoly period ended in most of Telefónica's concessions, competitors entered the market and offered consumers more choice, so the firm's effort to sustain its brand position shifted to choice and working hard to be consumers' preferred option. As competition intensified and new specialist brands penetrated particular market segments, Telefónica changed to a two-pronged strategy that emphasized the irrelevance of choice when the brand is superior: 'Your best option – Always Telefónica'. The firm also invested in building a strong corporate image for its other businesses, including data transmission and cellular telephones.[14]

Domestic brands have achieved credibility and a good reputation in recent years, so the challenge now is to build up an emotional response. With plant closures and economic uncertainty, Latin American consumers wonder whether their favorite domestic brands will disappear from the market, so firms should constantly reassure their customers of their long-term viability. Future success depends on the ability of brands to deliver a sense of security, warmth, self-respect and social approval.

The final building block is brand resonance and striving for enduring customer loyalty. Economic uncertainty may drive Latin American consumers to shop more infrequently, reduce product use or cease to purchase products in certain categories, or they may switch to other brands in search of better value. Thus firms must operate extremely effectively at every point of customer contact, for example by exploiting automated customer relationship technologies. Another important part of building brand resonance is aligning brand identification with consumers' beliefs and aspirations. Latin American consumers are increasingly demanding transparency and honesty in their relationship with firms, but very few firms have paid attention to this. Specialists have a better chance of establishing brand resonance because of their focused vision and single-brand image.

Brand strategy must be tailored to the country and market segment in question, especially in the case of resonance and meaning. At the lower level of brand building salience is achieved by a high degree of exposure in the mass media. Television is a major source of information and entertainment for most Latin American households. Close to 95 per cent of households have a TV set and watch it for four hours a day on average.[15] Firms' choice of advertising slot should be based on national preferences for certain types of program. For instance Chileans prefer movies and Mexicans favor entertainment programs. In Brazil and Venezuela children's programs have large audiences, as do sports programs in Argentina and international news in Colombia (Audits and Surveys, 1998).

With regard to eliciting an emotional response, this should be strictly tailored to the national culture. A successful example of this is provided by the Brazilian company Bombril, a manufacturer and marketer of household products. The company has used a character called the 'Bombril kid' in its advertisements for 23 years. The brand is kept fresh and relevant by having the character address controversial social or political issues in Brazil and the world, and the brand image is kept realistic by admitting in the message that as human beings we are all bound to make mistakes.[16]

Telecommunications and the media

To reach Latin American markets it is necessary to analyze the patterns of media use. New technologies and deregulation have invigorated the media and telecommunication sectors and attracted new players. In most countries the telecommunication infrastructure has been expanded and modernized. As a result firms have many more channels through which to reach consumers. Latin Americans are not only enjoying a greater choice of local programs, but with the globalization of the media and entertainment industry they are also exposed to international programs and programs from other Latin American countries. Thus a regional platform for topical issues is in the making. In this section we explore the penetration of telecommunications and other media, both new and traditional (Table 2.5).

Telecommunications

Telecommunications was one of the first sectors to be privatized and deregulated in Latin America, although the timing and approach varied from country to country. In Mexico a private monopoly was established for a set period of time, while in Argentina a duopoly of non-overlapping territories was created. During the early stages telecommunication companies concentrated on expanding and modernizing their networks. As a consequence the number of households with land-line telephones increased from 35 per cent in 1994 to almost 50 per cent in 1998 in Argentina, Chile, Venezuela and Colombia.

In Argentina, Chile and Mexico the monopoly set up in the first stage of privatization has ended and the sector is open to free competition. New services such as wireless telephony and the provision of internet access have become the focus of market competition. Unlike in advanced countries, where cellular phones serve as a complement to land-line phones, in Latin America they are the only option for households that cannot afford the telephone installation fee or are beyond the reach of the network. In the late 1990s the annual growth rate for cellular phones was 45 per cent, compared with just 11 per cent for land-line phones. Moreover market competition has since resulted in a lowering of subscription and call charges, making cellular phones more affordable and boosting demand.

Another reason for the popularity of cellular phones is related to the changes in lifestyle and family structure in Latin America. As discussed earlier, Latin American families are working more and leading busier lives as a result of economic crisis and uncertainty. In this situation cellular phones are ideal for keeping in touch with family members.

At the end of 2000 there were 58 million cellular phone subscribers in Latin America. In countries with greater market competition and more modern lifestyles, such as Chile, Mexico and Brazil, the number of subscribers has surpassed that of land-line subscribers. For example at the end of 2001 in Chile there were 4.37 million cellular phone subscribers and 3.65 land-line subscribers (*El Mercurio*, 24 March 2001; see also *InfoAmericas*, January 2001).

Table 2.5 Possession of and access to communication technologies, Latin America, 1999 (percentage of households)

	Landline telephones	Mobile telephones	One TV set	Two or more TV sets	Multichannel TV	Computer	Access to computer at work or school	Internet access
Argentina	49	13	99	44	67	17	6.0	6.0
Brazil	39	8	96	51	9	12	5.8	5.8
Chile	56	3	98	61	36	8	5.6	5.6
Colombia	66	4	97	42	50	9	5.0	5.0
Mexico	41	2	96	44	16	9	4.8	4.8
Venezuela	46	15	93	45	15	12	4.1	4.1
All Latin America	43	7	94	46	21	11	5.0	5.0
US Latinos	n.a.	31	97	n.a.	54	28	n.a.	24.0

Sources: Audits and Surveys (1999); Strategy Research Corporation (2000).

Television

Television is the principal source of information and entertainment in Latin America and the average Latin American household watches 4.87 hours of TV per day. The size and passion of this captive audience has given rise to powerful media groups such as Brazil's Globo, Mexico's Televisa and Venezuela's Venevision. The *telenovela* is one of the most popular program genres and on average attracts one third of the total audience on any given day.[17] Some of these programs are broadcast across the region and have become icons of Latin American culture.

Many Latin American households now have two or more TV sets, and in Chile and Brazil the proportion is more than 50 per cent. This is a reflection not only of growing affluence but also the variety of viewing preferences within households. As Table 2.6 shows, entertainment programs and movies are very popular and on the average Latin Americans devote 41 per cent of their viewing time to these genres. Programs for children, news and international programs follow in terms of viewing preference. Surprisingly, sports, music and family programs receive the lowest audience figures.

As noted earlier there are substantial differences in viewing preferences across countries. For instance Chileans prefer movies to any other type of program whereas Mexicans prefer comedy programs, Colombians are more interested in international programs and Venezuelans in programs for children. In the case of sports programs, Argentineans, Mexican and Brazilians have a passion for soccer but Venezuelans, Panamanians and Puerto Ricans prefer baseball. Even within a given sport, some versions attract viewers whereas others do not. Brazilian soccer is popular in many countries but Mexican soccer is difficult to promote. In addition local accents and the use of local slang prevent the regionalization of certain programs, such as comedy and music. Viewing differences are also marked within countries. For instance preferences differ between São Paulo and Rio de Janeiro in Brazil, Bogota and Cali in Colombia, and Mexico City and Monterrey in Mexico. While there is region-wide acceptance of relatively standardized programs such as CNN and MTV Latina, on average the two combined only account for 16 per cent of viewing time.[18]

Multichannel television has been gaining ground in Latin America. This provides alternatives to traditional TV broadcasts and encompasses cable TV, direct-to-home TV (satellite), small master antenna TV and multipoint distribution services. The large potential regional audience and the opening up of the market through licensing have attracted

Table 2.6 TV viewing hours and preferences, Latin America, 1999

	Average viewing hours per day	Share of viewing by type of program (%)								
		Entertainment	Movies	Children's programs	International	News	Documentaries	Sports	Music	Family
Argentina	4.87	23	15	11	10	15	7	10	4	4
Brazil	5.05	26	15	18	8	10	6	10	6	0
Chile	4.76	21	33	13	10	3	8	6	4	2
Colombia	4.10	18	13	10	33	5	7	3	8	3
Mexico	3.83	36	17	11	6	6	11	8	6	1
Venezuela	5.04	17	15	19	13	10	10	6	9	2
Average Latin America	4.87	24	17	13	13	10	8	8	6	2

Source: Audits and Surveys (1999).

investors and operators to the region. In 1994–98 multichannel TV grew at the rate of 34 per cent. By far the most popular among investors is cable TV because the technology is more mature, network expansion is more predictable and in some countries the regulatory framework is very transparent (Audits and Surveys, 1999). Cable TV companies generally focus on affluent urban areas, but in countries with more favorable conditions there is more extensive penetration. In 1999 67 per cent of households in Argentina and 50 per cent in Mexico had multichannel TV, which was comparable to the situation in more industrialized countries. With technological advances cable TV has become a conduit to other forms of telecommunication, such as telephony and the internet. Obviously cable TV companies are likely to become powerful rivals to traditional telecommunication operators providing similar services.

The internet[19]

Compared with the United States, internet access is quite low in Latin America. Latino internet users in the United States prefer English language websites and do not visit Spanish-only ones. US firms that target the Latin American market, however, offer bilingual options. For example Chase Bank has a bilingual site for its financial products and services. Bilingual capability also extends to other platforms, such as ATMs, call centers and direct marketing programs.[20]

Internet use in Latin America is still the domain of the affluent consumers, although it is expected to spread significantly at a compound annual growth rate of 47 per cent over the coming years, fuelled by interest from technologically aware young people, higher television penetration, improved telecommunication provision, the lowering or removal of connection charges and a reduction in the cost of personal computers (Landers, 2001). Estimates of the total number of internet users vary widely. The IDC put the number at 15 million in 2000 and predicted that more than 75 million people would have access by 2005 (*Mercurio*, 4 April 2001). Crèdit Suisse estimated in 2001 that there were 16 million users and uptake would grow at an annual rate of 39 per cent (Landers, 2001). Jupiter Research Latin American predicted that the number would increase from 21 million in 2000 to 77 million in 2005.[21] Finally, Morgan Stanley Dean Witter estimated in 2000 that households accounted for 37 per cent of total internet use in Latin America (Meeker *et al.*, 2000). Internet use will continue to be restricted among those in the poorer socioeconomic groups and in areas where telecommunication provision is underdeveloped.

Internet users in Latin America fall into four groups: infrequent users who access the internet for informational purposes, frequent business users who look for business-related information, home users who visit for information and entertainment purposes, and affluent teenage students who visit chat rooms.[22] Many internet users in Latin America read online newspapers or magazines (44 per cent), visit sites run by the government or educational institutions (37 per cent) and visit news or sports sites (32 per cent).[23] The typical Latin American internet shopper is male and in his late twenties (74 per cent). Most shoppers state that saving time is the main reason for shopping on the internet, followed by the ability to buy products that are not available in stores, better prices and brands, and better product information. The top five product categories purchased on the internet are software, books, music, magazine subscriptions and accessories for personal computers (Meeker *et al.*, 2000).

The average time spent on the internet rose from 8.2 hours a week in 1998 to 10.4 hours in 2000. Fifty per cent of home internet users have a connection speed of 56 kbps or faster, which is the standard in the United States. The majority of internet users in Latin America have dial-up access but 65 per cent would like to be able to connect via a cellular phone or pager and 13 per cent already have access via a mobile device. Only 10 per cent access the internet via television, although 67 per cent would do so if it were an option.[23]

E-commerce transactions are expected to increase at a compound annual growth rate of 117 per cent. In 2000 business-to-consumer (B2C) spending in Latin America was about US$226 million and business-to-business (B2B) spending was almost US$645 million (Landers, 2001). E-commerce in Latin America is limited by the low rate of credit card possession. The inefficiency of the national postal systems requires the use of expensive private delivery services. The lack of a customer service culture, high taxes and customs duties, and privacy and credit card security concerns are also serious issues of concern.

Competition among internet service providers (ISPs) is fierce. The monthly charges have plummeted and free internet access has been common. Banco Bradesco, Brazil's leading retail bank, began to offer its customers up to 20 hours of free access in December 1999. This resulted in it opening up to 2000 internet accounts per day and jolting other major retail banks in the region to do the same, or at least to offer online banking services (EIU, 2000). Several ISPs quickly followed suit, including InternetGratis, BRFree, Super11, Netgratuita and Catolico (sponsored by the Catholic Church). Universo Online in Brazil added a free service to its pay service, and Terra Networks began to offer free services across the region. The crash of the technological boom has ended the free service option and most ISPs are now shifting to subscription accounts.

Given the high telecommunication costs in the region, the end of free access is restricting the growth of the internet. With metered calls, Latin American internet users have to pay the charge levied on local telephone calls or on each minute of internet access. In Mexico users pay per local call, whereas in Argentina and Brazil they pay by the minute. In 2001 this added approximately US$3 in Mexico, US$9 in Brazil and US$17 in Argentina to the monthly fixed cost of US$26, US$21 and US$36 respectively (Landers, 2001).

Considering the large differences in culture and buying power, regional approaches to service provision have not always been successful. Two types of internet competitor have emerged: pan-regional and local market players. Pan-regional players spread their online services, content and infrastructure over several countries. Important players in this group are El Sitio, Terra Networks, Universo Online and the US-based StarMedia, Yahoo! and AOL. Local market players tailor their content and services to one country, as Ciudad does in Argentina. Even though portals require scale in order to be competitive, Latin American internet users demand local content. While the online language for South America is Spanish, except in Brazil, major linguistic and cultural differences between countries can make content developed for one country inappropriate for another.

Retailing

Modernization, new retail technology, the entry of global players and consolidation have changed the face of retailing in Latin America.

Self-service retailing

The spread of self-service retail outlets is the result of modernization and demographic transformation in Latin America.[24] The largest numbers of self-service stores are found in Argentina, Brazil and Chile. The drivers of retail transformation in these countries are consolidation, greater use of information technology and expansion to second- and third-tier metropolitan markets. In other countries, such as Mexico, Colombia and Peru, traditional shops remain the most important type of outlet. With the exception of Brazil, the level of penetration of supermarkets corresponds to the pattern of demographic transformation.

Argentina and Chile are at an advanced stage in this regard while Mexico and Colombia are reaching full transformation. Brazil is the exception because European retailers introduced self-service and discount stores to the country in the 1970s.

The market potential of self-service stores in Latin America depends on household buying power, the proportion of the household budget spent on food, and the size of the market. As discussed earlier, on average 35 per cent of household expenditure is on food. Expenditure is higher than the regional average in Argentina, Chile, Peru and Venezuela, and lower in Brazil and Mexico. In the case of household buying power, since food accounts for such a large part of consumption expenditure, per capita expenditure in supermarkets is a good indicator of self-service market potential. It is estimated that the average Latin American household spends US$161 per month on food. Argentine households have the highest per capita expenditures US$232, followed by Chilean households with individual food expenditure of US$179. Expenditure in the largest consumer market in Latin America, Brazil, is a low US$144. Thus it can be concluded that the retail sector in urban Argentina is the most developed retail sector in Latin America.

Global retailers

Early retail investors in Latin America were general merchandisers such as Sears, J. C. Penney, Carrefour and Makro. The French retail giant Carrefour was one of the first to move into the region. It entered Brazil in 1975 and Argentina in 1982.[25] Having secured its position in these countries, in 1994 it expanded its operations and opened two European-style hypermarkets in Mexico City in a joint venture with the domestic retailer Gigante. However the timing of its entry was unfortunate in that the devaluation of Mexican peso in the same year had a detrimental effect on the retail sector for the next couple of years.

The second wave of global retailers entered the region in the early to mid-1990s. These were mainly discount stores and product category specialists. They based their entry strategies on efficiency, supported by cutting edge information technology and full integration of the supply chain. The period was characterized by joint venture formation and the establishment of strategic alliances. One successful example was Wal-Mart's joint venture with Mexico's leading retailer, CIFRA, in 1991. The timing could not have been better as the prospects for the Mexican economy looked extremely favorable due to its imminent membership in NAFTA. In 1997 Wal-Mart acquired a controlling stake in CIFRA and expanded its super center chain to other parts of the country.

Encouraged by its successful entry to the Mexican market, Wal-Mart entered Puerto Rico in 1992, Argentina in 1994 and Brazil in 1995. The US retail giant attempted to replicate the successful Mexican joint venture experience in Brazil by forming a joint venture with Lojas Americanas in 1995. Subsequent expansion on its own into the Argentine market was initiated in 1999. However the company has had considerable difficulty replicating its Mexican success in Brazil and Argentina (EIU, 1999). Its problems in Argentina can be partially attributed to its discount stores stocking predominantly non-food merchandise in a country with a high per capita food expenditure, and to poor public reception of the club membership format of the Sam's Clubs. In contrast to Mexico, where Wal-Mart has built up a network of 27 discount stores and 28 Sam's Clubs, in Argentina it has only been able to establish 15 discount stores and three Sam's Clubs (*World Trade*, February 1999).

In the late 1990s many European retailers entered Latin America. For example the Portuguese company Sonae and Jerónimo Martins acquired several Brazilian regional retail chains, the French retailer Promodes collaborated with Argentina's Exxel Investment fund to acquire Norte and Tia, Casino of France formed a strategic partnership with Brazil's Pão de Açúcar,[26] and the Dutch retailer Ahold took a minority equity position in Disco of Argentina and Bompreço of Brazil. Meanwhile the earlier entrants continued to expand and to enter new countries. For instance Carrefour penetrated Colombia by setting up a joint venture with Bavaria, a large diversified family group.[27]

Domestic retail chains reacted to the entry of global retailers by acquiring new retail and supply chain technologies and renovating their stores to offer a more modern shopping experience. Some received financial resources and retail technology from global retailers that were willing to take a minority equity position. Others diversified into other services, such as travel and consumer credit.

One example of successful transformation is provided by Pão de Açúcar of Brazil. Fighting its way back from the brink of financial collapse in the early 1990s, Pão de Açúcar made radical changes in order to compete with the French chain Carrefour. It invested in all aspects of retail operations, ranging from logistics to customer response systems. It also centralized core activities such as purchasing and distribution, introduced category management systems and increased its range of own-label brands. To finance store expansion it tapped international capital markets and secured a US$1.5 billion capital infusion from the French retailer Casino in exchange for equity participation (*MMR*, September 1999). The acquisition of regional retail chains allowed the group to establish a presence throughout the enormous Brazilian territory. In the span of two years it opened 110 stores in various locations, and by 2000 it had revenues of US$4.8 billion and an impressive 13.5 per cent market share (Rosenburg, 2001).

Other new entrants were more specialist in nature, including Home Depot, which opened its first Latin American store in Chile in 1998, and Tower Records, which set up franchises in large metropolitan areas in the region.

With the worldwide economic slowdown during the early years of the twenty-first century the convenience consumer segment in Latin America experienced rapid growth. Given the absence of global players in this sector, domestic firms were able to secure the market niche. One such is Mexico's Elektra, a retailer of consumer electronic equipment and appliances targeting the low-income consumer segment. Elektra benefited from the latter's increased buying power when the Mexican economy was positively affected by the robust growth of the US economy in 1998–2000. It also entered a number of Central American markets with moderate success. Another example is Chile's Farmacias Ahumada, a pharmaceutical chain that has built up an extensive network in Latin America. It has 157 stores in Chile, 74 in Brazil and 45 in Peru.[28]

Retail consolidation

Retail consolidation in Latin America has occurred mostly at the national level. One reason for this was the need to achieve sufficient scale to support the large investments in new information, retail and supply chain technologies required to compete with the growing number of global retailers in the region. Several domestic retail chains acquired other chains in their countries by means of acquisition. As discussed in the previous section, others benefited from resources provided by international investors and strategic partners.

Retail strategies for the future

Brand strategies lay at the heart of effective retail strategies. There are two options for own-label brands: single brands for all types of outlet, regardless of the socioeconomic class being targeted, or different brands for different outlets and target groups. Latin American retailers have tended to favor the latter. For instance the largest supermarket chain in Chile, Distribución y Servicio, has developed four brands and two retail formats (supermarket and hypermarket) to cater separately to two socioeconomic groups (ABC1 and C2–3). By contrast the Chilean chain Santa

Isabel has a single brand and caters to the middle and lower socioeconomic classes in all types of outlet (supermarket, hypermarket and convenience stores).

A single format promotes shopping efficiency and customer relations. Consumers become familiar with store layouts and own-label brands, and can take advantage of store promotions regardless of location. In the United States, Wal-Mart has been experimenting with the concept of neighborhood markets, tentatively named Market Express. In Latin America the Colombian supermarket Carulla-Vivero is testing the small supermarket format in the northern part of the country. Specialist retailers and service sector companies should also succeed with a single brand strategy if they focus on a single market niche, as discussed earlier in this chapter.

Another component of future strategies should be to centralize core functions – customer response systems, consumer credit, merchandising – and so on and share them with suppliers, customers, alliance partners and employees. Such sharing can enhance the retail customer experience.

Pan-regional expansion will depend on the ability of the firm to replicate the above factors in other countries. Effective replication is possible in countries with a similar retail infrastructure and government regulations. In this regard, retail strategies based on the use of information systems are most appropriate for neighboring countries such as Chile, Argentina, Uruguay and Brazil. Retail regulations, on the other hand, can reduce the exportability of a retail format to other countries, and even within a country as regulations on location and opening hours tend to be enforced by local governments. Thus regulations can affect expansion from first- to second-tier city markets in the case of certain store formats, such as hypermarkets and other large stores.

The final dimension of future retail strategy is establishing direct contact with customers. The transformation of the Latin American retail industry has reduced customer influence on retailers. Manufacturers are trying to win back some of their influence on consumers by experimenting with ways to reach consumers directly. Nestlé is doing this with food categories that are likely to attract a sufficiently large number of customers. In Argentina it has opened small stores under the brand Frigor that exclusively sell Nestlé ice creams and coffee. The small store format can be used in various locations, such as within hypermarkets or in streets with a high volume of pedestrian traffic. A similar approach has been adopted by the Argentine brewery CCU, which has opened beer bars that sell only special beers.

Latin American markets in the twenty-first century

This chapter has described how global financial shocks, demographic shifts and technological developments are altering the social fabric of and consumer markets in Latin America. Although the structure of the family and lifestyles are changing, the family is still the center of social and consumption activities. Family members are working more hours but are not necessarily earning more money, and many have experienced a reduction of their buying power. Hence their overriding priority is value for money. As a result of market liberalization consumers now have much more choice, especially in large urban areas where companies have focused their investment efforts, so the challenge for competing firms is to offer the best possible value for money. However, given the instability of Latin American economies setting the right price can be difficult as conditions are constantly changing.

Another conclusion that has emerged from the analysis is that when conditions are unfavorable the markets adjust rapidly, but it can take several years for consumers to regain their confidence and return to their previous levels of consumption. This highlights the danger of using linear extrapolations based on periods of rapid growth to predict future sales. Firms that base their investment decisions on such predictions are vulnerable to overcapacity in the future.

The analysis of market segments in Latin America has shown that the market is fluid and fragmented. The conventional approach of using socioeconomic class to identify target groups is not enough to develop a sustainable business strategy unless the intention is to be a niche marketer. Educational level, professional status and connectivity via cohabitation seem to be better indicators of consumption patterns. The fact that social economic changes brought about by education and connectivity determine shifts in social class structures suggests some degree of mobility in society. Thus the implication for firms is that positioning should be based on enabling success through the ability to take into account such social mobility. This approach should also be consistent with the finding that consumers are becoming more cost conscious.

The reduction of the size of the middle class poses a challenge to firms that have based their strategies on the expected growth of this market segment. Hence non-niche, mass market firms must strive to attract customers from all segments with offerings that are acceptable to all.

Are the Latin American markets suitable for a regional strategic approach? Given the diversity of demographics, consumer preferences and consumption styles, this question has no simple answer. Much depends on the product category in question and the extent of its consumption in the countries concerned. One thing that all countries have in common is that consumer demand is based on the value for money concept. Inter-country differences can be simplified by nesting or layering market conditions. Markets can then be clustered and marketers can develop a tailored strategy for each cluster. In recent years multinational firms have based their strategies and operations on trading blocs such as MERCOSUR or NAFTA. However as pointed out in this chapter the countries in these blocs have not necessarily reached the same degree of demographic transformation. For example, from a demographic perspective Brazil has more in common with Mexico, Colombia and Peru than with its partners in MERCOSUR. Hence a marketing strategy that treats Brazil, Uruguay and Argentina (all MERCOSUR members) as one group may not be effective. Rather grouping countries according to their degree of demographic transformation (see Figure 2.1) and the lifestyle segmentation of their consumers may be a more effective way to approach markets in Latin America. Depending on the product category, other combinations may be more effective. The main point is that Latin American markets are complex and multidimensional, and firms that are able to unravel this complexity will succeed.

3
Marketing in Brazil

Map 2   Brazil
Source: www.lib.utexas.edu/maps/cia04/brazil_sm04.gif.

Brief historical background

Brazil has been inhabited for more than 30 000 years. The indigenous Indian people were few and scattered. They were originally hunters but later engaged in crop production and animal breeding.

The Portuguese explorer Pedro Alvares Cabral landed with his men on the Brazilian coast in 1500 AD, and in 1532 Portuguese colonizers founded São Vincente, the first settlement on Brazilian soil. Subsequently Dutch and French settlements were established in north-eastern Brazil, but the Portuguese launched attacks on them and gained full control of the region.

Gradually a feudal system developed, based on the ownership of huge sugar cane plantations called *capitanias*. Initially the landowners relied exclusively on native Indian labor but the rapid growth of agriculture soon necessitated a much larger labor force so millions of slaves were imported from Africa.

Inland settlements, *Quilombos*, began to be set up at the end of the seventeenth century by slaves who had escaped from the plantations. There were continuous clashes between the inhabitants of the *Quilombos* and troops sent by landowners to force the slaves back to the plantations. In the process most of the settlements were destroyed.

At the beginning of the eighteenth century gold and diamonds were discovered in Minas Gerais, resulting in the gradual development of the interior. In 1763 the main settlement of the colony was moved from Bahia to Rio de Janeiro. During the period 1807–8 the king of Portugal, João VI, who had fled from the Napoleonic invasion, took refuge in Rio de Janeiro and Brazil underwent spectacular economic development as the seat of the Portuguese monarchy and government. Portuguese rule had a major influence on Brazil's traditions, language, culture and national identity.

From the beginning of the nineteenth century the population of Brazil engaged a bid for independence. The Portuguese royal court eventually conceded to Brazil's independence in 1822 and the country became an empire, ruled by the son of the king. (This was unique in that all the other colonies in North and South America became republics after their independence.) The emperor ruled Brazil erratically and involved it in a devastating war with Argentina that lasted from 1825 to 1828. This was followed in 1831 by social unrest in Rio de Janeiro, which forced the emperor to abdicate in favor of his son, Pedro II, the second and last Brazilian emperor. He implemented many reforms and abolished slavery in 1887. Meanwhile millions of Europeans, mainly from Italy, Germany and Poland, were encouraged to migrate to southern Brazil in search of a better life. Brazil's involvement in numerous conflicts with neighboring countries led to the overthrow of the monarchy and the establishment of a republic in 1889.

The Brazilian economy was entirely based on agriculture. At the end of the nineteenth century the industrial demand for rubber created a boom in rubber production, but it was short lived and the focus shifted to coffee bean production, which became the country's principal export. In 1930 Getúlio Dornelles Vargas led a rebellion that ousted the government. President Vargas ruled Brazil as a benevolent dictator for the next 15 years, during which time industrialization was encouraged by economic reforms in the private and public sectors.

Brazil joined the Second World War on the side of the Allies. Immediately after the war Vargas was forced to resign by the military. In 1950 he was returned to power, but this time his rule was controversial, with many scandals and serious economic hardships, which forced him to resign in 1954, shortly afterwards he committed suicide.

Vargas's successor, Juscelino Kubitschek, took it upon himself to boost the economic development of the interior of the country, and to this end the decision was made to create a new purpose-built capital. Thus in 1960 Brasília became the capital of Brazil.

The subsequent presidency of João Goulart was leftist and seemed to be growing more and more pro-communist, prompting a military coup in 1964. Successive military regimes ruled Brazil until 1985. They promoted economic growth by encouraging domestic business development. Meanwhile civil rights were suppressed, the constitution was suspended and censorship was imposed. The industrialization of the country intensified in the late 1960s and 1970s, thus changing the structure of the economy. The expansion of industry created thousands of new jobs and the sector became a major contributor to GDP.

Shortly after the end of military rule the powerful politician José Sarney became president and a democratic constitution was adopted in 1988. The next year Fernando Collor de Mello took office and implemented ambitious programs called *pacotes* (packages) to curb inflation and government spending. However corruption flourished and de Mello was impeached and forced to step down in 1992.

Itamar Franco served as president until 1995, when he was replaced by Fernando Henrique Cardoso. The latter implemented measures to generate economic growth, bring down inflation and stabilize the national currency. He privatized many state-owned businesses, including telecommunications, mining, oil and electricity. The service sector flourished and became an important contributor to GDP. Because of his sound economic policies Cardoso was reelected, but a subsequent economic crisis resulted in currency devaluation and high interest rates.

Helped by an IMF aid package of US$42 billion, Brazil adhered to a strict fiscal policy that brought about economic stabilization. However continuous corruption scandals were followed by a severe energy crisis. Social dissatisfaction with the economic austerities led to the election of Lula da Silva, who promised to reduce unemployment and introduce social reforms to improve the living standards of the poor.

Population

In 2004 it was estimated that Brazil's population amounted to 184 million, or more than one third of the population of Latin America. In terms of population, Brazil is the fifth largest country in the world, following China, India, the United States, and Indonesia. Its ethnic structure is extremely diverse because of the mixing of European colonizers and immigrants with indigenous inhabitants and Africans forcefully brought to the country as slaves. Currently about 55 per cent of Brazilians are white, 9 per cent are black, 35 per cent are of mixed origin and 1 per cent are of Asian decent. Portuguese is the official language, but English, French and Spanish are widely spoken. Roman Catholicism is the religion of more than 90 per cent of the people.

Life expectancy has improved over the last two decades and currently stands at 68 years. The proportion of older people has been increasing since 1970 and that of young people under the age of 14 has been falling (Figure 3.1).

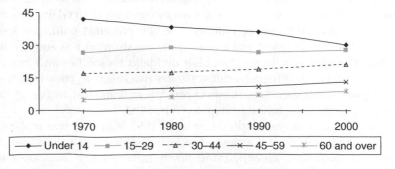

Figure 3.1 Age structure of the Brazilian population, 1970–2000 (per cent)
Source: Instituto Brasileiro de Geografia e Estatística.

Brazil is divided into five regions with similar sociodemographic and economic characteristics: Central-western, North-eastern, Northern, South-eastern and Southern. The South-eastern region is economically well-developed and has a high population density, while the other regions are less developed and have low population densities. The Northern region mainly comprises the Amazon Basin, where few people live and there is almost no industry. The population is concentrated on the Atlantic coastline and alongside the largest rivers, mostly in towns and cities. A demographic breakdown of the regions is presented in Table 3.1.

Income distribution has been highly unequal for decades. The richest segment of society comprises just 1 per cent of the population but holds 18 per cent of the national wealth; the poorest segment comprises 52 per cent of the population and holds a mere 11 per cent of the national wealth. Most of the wealth is concentrated in the South-eastern region, while the North-eastern region has the lowest average per capita income in the country (Figure 3.2).

Table 3.1 Demographic characteristics of the Brazilian regions

	Percentage of total area	*Percentage of total population*	*Percentage of urban dwellers*	*Percentage of rural dwellers*
Central-western	19	7	87	13
North-eastern	18	28	66	34
Northern	45	7	70	30
South-eastern	11	43	92	8
Southern	7	15	80	20

Source: Instituto Brasileiro de Geografia e Estatística.

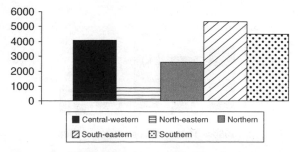

Figure 3.2 Average regional per capita income, Brazil, 2002 (US dollars)
Source: Instituto Brasileiro de Geografia e Estatística.

The share of women in the workforce has increased and by the end of 2003 they accounted for 44 per cent of the total workforce. This has had a significant impact on family income and lifestyle.

Economic overview

Brazil is one of the largest economies in the world. The economy was first based on agriculture and mining, and later supplemented by manufacturing and services. Brazil is the world's most important producer of coffee, sugar cane, bananas, cocoa, tobacco, cotton, corn, beef and soya beans, among others. There is an abundance of natural resources, including minerals such as iron ore, bauxite, nickel, gold, manganese, diamonds, uranium and platinum, as well as numerous reservoirs and forests and diverse species of flora and fauna. The largest rainforest in the world is in the Amazon region, which occupies about two thirds of the territory of Brazil. Manufacturing has been developing rapidly, with the production of textiles, shoes, food items, automobiles, planes and ships taking the lead. The manufacturing industry is strongly supported by the production of steel, crude oil, chemicals and agriculture.

GDP growth rates have varied according to changes in the economic system. It is interesting to note that when the government was using protectionist measures and an import substitution strategy to ensure the growth of domestic business, the GDP growth rates were much higher than when economic liberalization and privatization were implemented and FDI inflows increased (Figure 3.3).

The high inflation rates in the first half of the 1990s – inflation reached almost 2500 per cent in 1993 – deterred economic development,

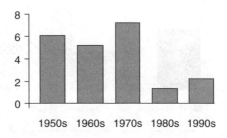

Figure 3.3 Average GDP growth, Brazil, 1950s–1990s (per cent)
Source: Instituto Brasileiro de Geografia e Estatística.

but since the introduction of the Real Plan the economy has stabilized, inflation has been kept under control and living standards have improved.

In 2003 GDP fell slightly by about 0.2 per cent, but per capita GDP dropped by more than 1.5 per cent as a result of population growth of 1.3 per cent. In 1994–2003 GDP growth averaged 2.4 per cent, which was lower than in the world's other large countries: China (8.3 per cent), India (5.9 per cent), the United States (3.2 per cent), and Indonesia (4.6 per cent), all of which had much larger populations. The annual changes in GDP and per capita GDP in 1994–2003 are shown in Figure 3.4.

The performance of the different economic sectors varied in 2003. The contribution of crop and livestock farming to GDP grew by 5 per cent, while those of industry and the service sector fell by 1 per cent and 0.1 per cent respectively. The contributions made by mining and manu-facturing rose slightly by 2.8 per cent and 0.9 per cent respectively, but there was a significant decrease of 8.6 per cent in the contribution of civil engineering. Commerce shrank substantially by 2.6 per cent. The overall contribution of the economic sectors to employment and GDP and the changes in this over time are shown in Figure 3.5.

Consumption began to fall in 2001 and gathered pace in 2003, when it fell by 3.3 per cent. At the same time government spending rose, with a 0.6 per cent increase in 2003. Consumption of both consumer and industrial goods was highest in the South-eastern and Southern regions, while the Northern region had the lowest consumption per capita.

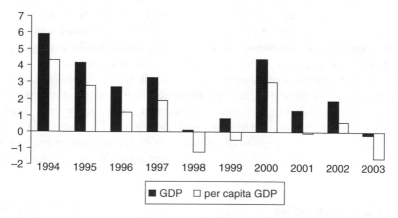

Figure 3.4 Annual changes in GDP and per capita GDP, 1994–2003 (per cent)
Source: Instituto Brasileiro de Geografia e Estatística.

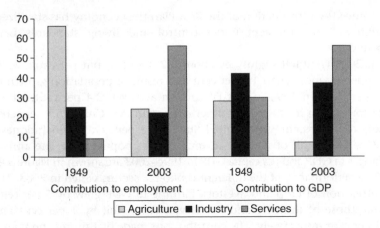

Figure 3.5   Contribution of the principal Brazilian economic sectors to employment and GDP, 1949 and 2003 (per cent)
Source: Adapted from data from the Instituto Brasileiro de Geografia e Estatística.

The economic situation began to look more optimistic in 2004. The Government Statistics Agency announced rises of 5.2 per cent in GDP and 3.8 per cent in per capita GDP. Because of its abundant resources Brazil was positively affected by the increased price of commodities, mainly iron ore and soya beans. This and the global economic revitalization in 2004 resulted in the value of exports rising by almost 18 per cent, leading to a significant trade surplus of US$33.7 billion.

According to the Brazilian National Confederation of Industry the pace of economic growth is likely to be sustained for several years to come, which will have a profound effect on the development of small and medium-sized businesses and their participation in the economy.

Brazil's international competitiveness has been improving since the early 1990s due to a number of factors, not least its natural resources, advanced telecommunications infrastructure and comparatively skilled workforce. In addition companies have been forced to become more competitive since foreign trade liberalization allowed the entry of foreign competitors. Finally, increased consumer demand has put pressure on companies to meet the needs of more sophisticated and demanding customers at home and abroad.

Brazilian companies

The gradual liberalization and stabilization of the Brazilian economy in the 1990s was accompanied by increased foreign trade, a massive inflow of capital and the enlargement of MERCOSUR (MERCOSUL in Portuguese), which created both opportunities and challenges for Brazilian companies. Having enjoyed strict protectionist measures for many decades, domestic firms were suddenly exposed to strong international competition that threatened their survival. A number of large and well-established leading companies in various industries, such as automobile and toy production, ceased to operate or were bought by giant foreign corporations.

Brazilian firms gradually came to terms with the new economic realities and engaged in industry consolidation via mergers and acquisitions. This gave rise to productivity improvements, cost reductions, quality improvement and greater emphasis on customer satisfaction.

In the 1990s Brazilian companies internationalized their operations on a massive scale. This was a difficult undertaking as they lacked experience and global brand recognition. Previously by the government's protectionist policy coupled with the enormous domestic market had discouraged local firms from going abroad and the country's location had not favored trade outside the Latin American region.

The major drivers of internationalization were the desire to grow through continuous expansion, the consolidation of existing operations abroad, the need to internationalize in order to survive, and the wish to explore opportunities overseas. The consolidation of domestic firms became the principal vehicle for international expansion and export growth. Many large Brazilian exporters recognized the need to be closer to their international clients. Consequently a number of firms expanded abroad by investing in international production and marketing operations. In 1994–99 the value of the Brazilian currency was high, and this encouraged an outflow of capital for the expansion of existing or the creation of new international operations. Firms made significant investments in the MERCOSUR countries and other countries in the region, and in high-growth markets all over the world.

Foreign trade

In Brazil foreign trade is regulated and managed by the Ministry of Industry, Commerce and Tourism, the Ministry of Foreign Relations and the Ministry of Finance. In addition several agencies engage in foreign trade activities under the leadership of the Chamber of Foreign Trade, which reports directly to the President's Office. Foreign trade almost doubled between 1993 and 2003. In 1994–2000 imports grew at an average of 10.9 per cent per annum but exports increased at the much lower rate of 4.3 per cent, thus generating a trade deficit. In

1995–96 this was exacerbated by appreciation of the exchange rate. However since 2000 exports have exceeded imports, which has had a positive impact on the trade balance. For example in 2003 exports amounted to US$73.1 billion and imports to US$48.3 billion, creating a surplus of US$24.8 billion (Figure 3.6).

In 2000 Brazil was ranked twenty-eighth on the list of the world's largest exporters by the World Trade Organization (WTO); in 2004 it was ranked twentieth. Brazilian exports consist mainly of primary and manufactured products based on natural resources to satisfy the growing demand in developed economies and the enormous requirements of Chinese manufacturers. In the case of Latin American markets, the importance of scale intensive goods (such as food products) has risen and R&D intensive products (such as personal computers) have been increasing.

The Brazilian government has attempted to diversify the structure of imports and exports since the mid-1990s. Agricultural products contribute strongly to total exports. For example in 1996–2000, 4 per cent of the volume of exports was accounted for by coffee, 3.5 per cent by soya beans and 2 per cent by raw cane sugar. Raw materials and capital goods accounted for most imports, averaging 76 per cent of the total value of imports in 1998–2000, followed by consumer goods (15 per cent), crude oil (4.5 per cent), automobiles (2.9 per cent) and natural gas (1.6 per cent).

Import policy underwent a major change in the 1990s, with a shift from import substitution to import liberalization. There was a constant reduction of import tariffs, with the average tariff falling from 32.2 per cent in 1990 to 12.4 per cent in 2000. From 1995 a common external tariff was enforced in the MERCOSUR countries, including Brazil. Higher

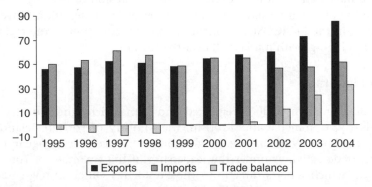

Figure 3.6 Foreign trade, Brazil, 1995–2004 (US$ billion)
Source: Ministry for Development, Industry and International Trade.

tariffs were applied to goods with higher value added. The Brazilian import system is in line with the requirements of the WTO Import Licensing Procedure Agreement. In 1997 the administrative import procedure was simplified by means of the Integrated Foreign Trade System (SISCOMEX). Brazil has banned the importation of used consumer goods, non-biological detergents and some pharmaceutical products, agricultural chemicals and animal feeds that are considered harmful. These restrictions are strictly enforced to safeguard the development of agriculture and protect the consumer goods sector against cheap, low-quality, used products.

Under the government's export promotion policy, exports are exempt from indirect taxes and credit assistance is provided by the National Bank for Economic and Social Development and the Banco do Brasil. Inputs for products destined for export also enjoy tariff exemption. In addition the export strategy encourages small and medium-sized companies to engage in export operations by offering them information on business opportunities.

The major trading partners of Brazil are the United States, the European Union and Japan, which together have accounted for more than 50 per cent of foreign trade over the past 15 years. The European Union has traditionally been a strong trading partner, with a share of 29 per cent of all transactions between 1998 and 2000. The United States had a 22 per cent share over the same period, with an increase in the value of Brazilian exports to the United States and a decrease in the value of export from the latter to Brazil. MERCOSUR accounted for 15 per cent and Asia for 13 per cent of trade. Argentina is Brazil's principal trading partner in the MERCOSUR bloc.

Brazil is committed to facilitating foreign trade and was one of the key initiators and supporters of measures to improve the opportunities for developing nations to contribute more significantly to world trade.

Foreign direct investment

Amendments to the Brazilian constitution in 1995 created the same conditions for the functioning of foreign and domestic companies. Consequently foreign companies can freely enter Brazil and receive national treatment. However there are still some restrictions on foreign investment in strategically important sectors such as nuclear energy, health services, rural property, fishing, postal services, aviation and aerospace.

Since 1996 the service sector has been the biggest recipient of FDI and on average has received about 80 per cent of the total FDI inflow. Industrial production (mainly electronics, automobiles, pharmaceuticals, processed food and rubber) has absorbed just 19 per cent, and FDI in the agricultural sector has been negligible. The major providers of foreign capital since the mid-1990s have been the United States and European Union countries, particularly, Spain, the Netherlands, France and Portugal. The inflows and outflows of FDI in 1996–2004 are shown in Figure 3.7.

In 1996 the inflow of FDI was 5.5 times higher than the FDI accumulated in 1990–95, and over the next five years there was a constant increase. While the worldwide economic slowdown caused a fall in FDI in 2001–3, in 2004 it started to increase again.

In 1997–2004 Brazil and Mexico attracted the bulk of FDI in Latin America. Each year Brazil received between 25.6 per cent and 35.1 per cent of the total regional inflow and between 54 per cent and 86 per cent of the inflow into the MERCOSUR countries. A substantial proportion of the FDI went into the purchase of large state-owned industrial and utility enterprises, such as manufacturing, electricity generation and telecommunications companies. In 1999 one third of FDI was allotted to such ventures, but this proportion fell considerably in 2001. The decrease was double that in other emerging markets worldwide and substantially higher than the average decrease of FDI in Latin America.

The inflow of capital gave a major boost to the internationalization of the Brazilian economy and intensified outward investment in 1996–2002. This upward trend was briefly interrupted in 2003, but in 2004 outward FDI from Brazil increased substantially.

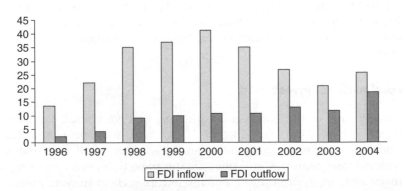

Figure 3.7   FDI, inflows and outflows, Brazil, 1996–2004 (US$ billion)
Source: Banco Central do Brasil.

The share of foreign firms in the total turnover of the 500 largest companies in Brazil increased from 27 per cent in 1989 to 56 per cent in 2000. Presently companies with foreign ownership account for half of the value of exports and two thirds of the value of imports. According to de Negri (2003), firms with foreign ownership are generally larger, more productive and have a greater marketing orientation than domestic companies. They spend a larger amount on upgrading the qualifications of their employees and promoting their products, especially in the business-to-consumer markets. Thus foreign companies enjoy strong competitive advantages in the domestic and export markets. However the spillover effects of the new business environment are enabling domestically owned enterprises to narrow the performance gap between them and foreign firms.

Consumer spending and buying behavior

The consumer market in Brazil is dynamic and growing. In 2002 total consumer expenditure was approximately US$310 billion, the largest in Latin America. Among the more than 50 million households there are large disparities in disposable income and purchasing power. Consumers in class A have an average household monthly income of US$3000, in contrast to an income of US$900 for class B, US$350 for class C and just US$100 for classes D and E. In 2003 class D and E consumers accounted for more than 50 per cent of the population but had only 10 per cent of the purchasing power. The situation was more balanced in the case of class C consumers, who amounted to 29 per cent of the population and had 25 per cent of the total buying power. However class B consumers (14.3 per cent of the population) and class A consumers (less than 3 per cent of the population) had disproportionately large shares of buying power of 35 per cent and 30 per cent respectively.

Consumer spending also differs along the urban–rural divide (Table 3.2). Consumers in urban areas have a much greater spending power and are more prone to be influenced by advertising than people in rural areas. TV and newspaper advertising and the internet are increasingly influencing urban consumption, while in some rural areas there is not even electricity.

Brazil is a country of huge contrasts in terms of buying behavior but the majority of consumers, although very price conscious, like to purchase well-established brands and expensive items. Many affluent customers consider it a matter of prestige to buy fashionable and luxury products.

Table 3.2   Regional urban and rural consumption, Brazil, 2001

	Urban population as a percentage of the total population	Urban areas' percentage share of the total consumption potential	Rural population as a percentage of the total population	Rural areas' percentage share of the total consumption potential
Central-western	6	7	1	0.2
North-eastern	18	14	10	1.5
Northern	5	4	2	0.6
South-eastern	40	59	3	1.3
Southern	12	12	3	0.4
All Brazil	81	96	19	4.0

Source: Author's calculations based on data from the Instituto Brasileiro de Geografia e Estatística.

Brazil has a reputation as the fashion capital of Latin America. In São Paolo and Rio de Janeiro high-income consumers can buy top international fashion brands such as Armani, Prada and Versace. Equally well regarded are the many Brazilian fashion brands that reflect the inventive, lively, multicolored and nature-inspired culture of the country. They are sold in specialty shops whose decor is a carefully chosen blend of modern and indigenous design. High-income customers who shop for exclusive clothes, jewelry, furniture, accessories and cosmetics favor boutiques and stores with an atmosphere of exclusivity. High-fashion items are also sold in fashion centers where both international and Brazilian brands are available. One of the largest and best of these is Morumbi of São Paolo, which houses more than 400 fashion boutiques selling European, US and Brazilian brands (Kaufman, 2004). Because of Brazilians' colonial past and sense of belonging, domestic and European brands are favored over US ones.

In the case of general items and food, the impact of the economic crisis has made Brazilians more concerned about value for money and they have shifted their attention to cheaper brands. Brand awareness is stronger in highly urbanized areas. Buyers shop from a variety of outlets. Class A and B consumers prefer shopping centers, supermarkets and hypermarkets. While lower-income consumers tend to buy from small retailers, open markets and street sellers, the larger supermarket and hypermarket chains have introduced lower-cost products and special offers in order to attract all socioeconomic classes. Supermarkets now account for about two thirds of total food revenue, although households tend to supplement their purchases with food from specialist and traditional stores. On the whole consumer loyalty tends to be in terms of producers and brands rather than retail outlets. The overall consumption pattern in Brazil resembles those in other emerging markets, where food items account for about two thirds of retail income.

Advertising plays a major part in purchasing decisions in urban areas. People in classes A and B are mainly influenced by advertisements in newspapers and magazines, followed by advertisements on the radio. For food products, class C consumers are mostly influenced by TV commercials and to a lesser extent by advertisements on the radio and in the print media. Advertisements in the print media have little impact on class C, D and E consumers when it comes to buying consumer durables.

The impact of radio and print advertising is greater among those with higher educational and income levels. Buyers with low educational and income levels spend more hours watching television but their consumption expenditure is low and their buying pattern is traditional. Thus TV viewers from the lower socioeconomic classes tend to regard television commercials as entertainment.

While class A and B consumers have become sensitive to the benefits of healthy food the purchase of semiprocessed and ready-to-eat food has increased substantially.

As noted earlier, value for money has become an important factor in purchasing decisions. Due to the falling purchasing power of consumers in class C and the already low purchasing power of classes D and E, companies have introduced cheaper 'B brands', thus catering to the price sensitivity of consumers and taking market share from well-established international and global brands. For example the market share of the leader in cereals, Kellogg, fell from more than 75 per cent in 1996 to 47 per cent in 2002. A similar reduction in market share has been experienced by Nestlé, Coca-Cola and many other multinational corporations. By 2002 more than 30 per cent of all branded consumer goods sold in Brazil were B brands (Gouvea, 2004).

The industrial market

Despite the economic crisis the industrial market in Brazil grew in 1999–2003. In 2002 the total revenue from business-to-business sales rose by 16.7 per cent to US$10.7 billion. This increase was mostly accounted for by agricultural machinery, heavy duty construction equipment and textile machinery.

Exports of industrial goods continue to register a small annual increase, while traditional exports to the United States, Germany and Britain have experienced moderate growth. The Latin American market has shrunk, but exports to the large emerging markets of China, Russia, South Africa and India have been generally on the rise.

Imports of industrial goods have followed the overall trend of import decrease and on average fell by 15 per cent in 2001–3. This was due to the implementation of an import substitution program aimed at encouraging domestic producers to increase their market share. Thus in 2001 Brazilian manufacturers accounted for 52 per cent of the value of all industrial transactions in the country. This share increased to 64 per cent in 2002, further boosting the competitive advantage of Brazilian firms.

A major development has been the relocation of production facilities from the large urban centers on the coast to the interior of the country to take advantage of the cheaper raw materials and the availability of qualified workforce. Moreover inland local governments have provided many incentives for industry relocation. As most of the existing production facilities are obsolete there is a demand for modern industrial parks, giving a boost to the construction industry. The Brazilian Association for Industrial Machinery is optimistic about the prospects for industrial production in 2004–7, forecasting an annual average increase in demand of 15–18 per cent. This is based on the expectation that the government's new economic policy will boost industrial investment.

The food market

The majority of urban consumers buy food that is quick and easy to prepare, a habit that has become more typical with growing urbanization and the relocation of industry from the coastline to the interior of the country. Consequently super- and hypermarkets have begun to make space for cooked and ready-to-eat food. The number of fast food chains has also been on the rise since the mid-1980s.

Food sales, and especially sales of ready-to-eat food, are expected to grow significantly in 2005–10. Products with the highest growth potential are pizzas, prepared dishes of chicken and rice or beans, vegetable blends, and varieties of salads. Meals that are cheap and easily prepared are expected to enjoy immense growth. The food-processing industry in Brazil is the largest in Latin America and produces a broad range of goods. However the domestic supply is still insufficient to meet the rapidly growing demand for processed food, especially in the South-eastern region and a substantial proportion has to be imported (more than a fifth in 2003). The principal sources of imported food are Argentina, the United States and a number of European Union countries.

Food producers and suppliers include commodity specialists, domestic companies, international firms and large global corporations. Commodity specialists supply basic agricultural produce at low prices and with modest value added. They are small in scale, with annual sales of up to US$150 million. Larger companies of this type specialize in dairy products, sugar and oilseeds, and some have developed strong domestic brands. Well-established and financially viable regional commodity specialists have developed successful brands and aspire to national recognition.

The numerous companies engaged in brand building vary in size, scope and degree of internationalization. They are predominantly family-owned and compete with a single brand. Some of the most successful ones have been targeted by powerful global and international players that wish to acquire strong local brands in order to establish or expand their market presence in Brazil. Domestic companies with a good financial performance aspire to joint venture operations or strategic alliances with foreign players. Since the mid-1990s these companies have been continuously engaged in expanding their sales in the MERCOSUR countries, the rest of Latin America and beyond.

International companies operating in Brazil usually establish local production facilities, mostly by acquiring domestic firms and brands. Companies such as Bunge, Nabisco and Quaker Foods have developed a portfolio of national brands via successive acquisitions. In the food processing sector there is a strong presence by global corporations such as Kellogg, Kraft Foods, Nestlé and Unilever. Meanwhile Perdigão and Sadia – the leading Brazilian producers and distributors of processed, frozen and chilled food, including fresh and frozen pasta, pizzas, processed meat and fish dishes – are competing successfully with the global companies and are exporting worldwide.

The global brands established by Unilever and Nestlé command a high percentage of market share worldwide. Their experience in running production facilities and marketing in various countries has given them an advantage in the Brazilian market. Their product, promotional, distribution and pricing strategies are based on knowledge and experience accumulated in markets all over the world. Being more experienced and financially stronger than their domestic rivals, international and global food companies stand a better chance of increasing their market share in Brazil. However the appreciation of domestic food brands by all consumers, especially those in classes C and D gives a competitive edge to many local companies.

Due to economic volatility and inflation, for a long time prices were controlled by the Brazilian government through retail price ceilings, high taxes on imported food and special agricultural tariffs, thus limiting market-based pricing. However since economic liberalization in the mid 1990s prices have reflected market dynamics. These changes have increased the price sensitivity of Brazilian consumers.

Food consumption in Brazil tends to be along traditional lines, which has served to limit investment in new product development, as have past protectionist measures and high tariffs on machinery and equipment. Recently the reduction of tariffs has had a positive effect on the degree of innovation.

Key problems for food companies have been the highly fragmented distribution system, the vast territory of the country and limited refrigerated storage facilities, but joint ventures, strategic alliances and acquisitions have given them access to local distribution networks, wholesalers and retailers. The latter have considerable bargaining power because they account for the bulk of food sales while wholesalers focus on lower value-added foods. Considering that on average most of households' monthly income is spent on food, retailers play an important part in the economy. Restaurants are the least important branch of the Brazilian food industry in that they only generate about 10 per cent of the industry's revenue.

Retailing

Retailing in Brazil is complicated by the vast size of the country, the diverse consumer base, variations in consumer demand and preference in the various regions, the inconsistent growth rate of the economy and per capita GDP over the last two decades, and the economic crisis of the 1990s. However the growth of retail business has been aided by a significant number of informal retail operations and tax evasion.

While the devaluation of the Brazilian currency in 1998–99 had a positive impact on the growth of the retail sector, the global economic slowdown in 2001–3, the 2001 energy crisis in Brazil and the 2001–2 Argentine debt default led to a continuous fall in aggregate consumer demand. Buyers became more cautious about their purchases and demanded better value for money. It is expected that the establishment of the Free Trade Area of the Americas will facilitate more vigorous economic development in Brazil and lead to an increase in consumer demand.

Concentration and consolidation have been major trends in the development of Brazilian retailing in the last 15 years, prompted by growing competition, the entry and expansion of foreign retailers and the continuing rivalry between supermarkets and traditional retailers. In the process of retail restructuring traditional department stores lost some of their attractiveness and identity, which initially slowed the growth of their operations. Recently they have gone through a significant recovery in terms of turnover and popularity, mostly among class C consumers.

At the beginning of the twenty-first century there were approximately 24 000 supermarkets in Brazil, which was twice the number in 1991. As illustrated in Figure 3.8, the economic crises in the 1990s caused considerable fluctuations in the number of outlets, with many being forced to close. There has been extensive consolidation among domestic and foreign companies. For example the largest domestic supermarket chain, Pão de Açúcar, working in partnership with the French-owned retailer Casino, merged with the Sendas Group, which once controlled the retail sector in Rio de Janeiro. After the merger investments were made in expanding the chain and making service improvements with the aim of securing a huge increase in market share. Pão de Açúcar targets various socioeconomic groups. The company's own brand, Pão de Açúcar, is aimed at consumers with a relatively high disposable income and the stores are up-market. The brand Barateiro is targeted at low-income consumers and the brand Extra is sold in hypermarkets that mostly attract middle- and lower-class consumers.

The principal rival of Pão de Açúcar is the French retail giant Carrefour, which ranks second in terms of market share and has invested heavily

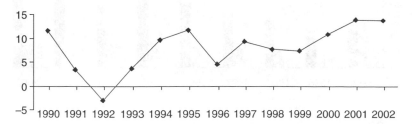

Figure 3.8 Annual change in the number of supermarket outlets, Brazil, 1989–2002 (per cent)
Source: AC Nielsen.

in new outlets and service improvement. In March 2004 the US Wal-Mart bought the retail chain Bompreço from the Dutch Ahold Group to become the third largest retailer in Brazil. The sales of the five largest retailers are shown in Table 3.3 and the market shares of Pão de Açúcar, Carrefour and the ten largest retailers are shown in Figure 3.9.

The structure of the retail sector is determined by the strong positions of Brazilian, French, US, Portuguese and Dutch retailers. The super- and hypermarket chains have played a major part in changing the purchasing habits of class A, B and C consumers since the mid 1990s. Some retailers, such as Pão de Açúcar, Carrefour and Sonae, have developed strong own brands.

The strategic approaches of domestic and foreign retailers differ. International retailers such as Carrefour and Wal-Mart are mainly concerned with logistics and distribution. Large food companies usually

Table 3.3 Value of sales by the five largest retailers, Brazil, 2004 (US$ billion)

	Ownership	Total sales
Pão de Açúcar	Brazilian/French	5.5
Carrefour	French	3.8
Wal-Mart	US	2.5
Cacas Bahia	Brazilian	2.0
Sonae	Portuguese	1.5

Note: Wal-Mart's sales include those of Bompreço.
Source: Adapted from www.v-brazil.com.

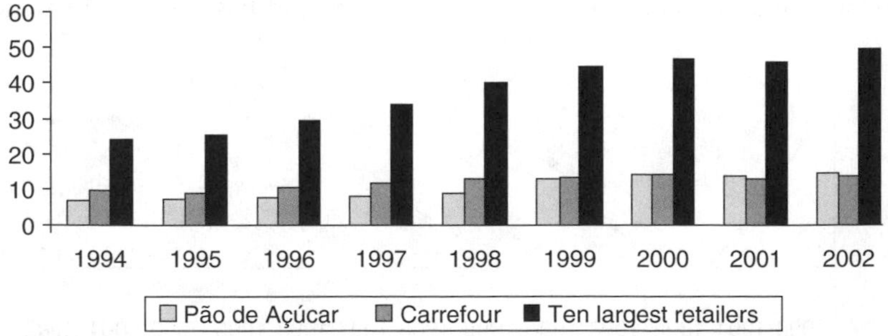

Figure 3.9 Market share of Pão de Açúcar, Carrefour and the ten largest retailers, Brazil, 1994–2002 (per cent)
Source: Brazilian Supermarket Association.

develop their own distribution networks with specialist distributors who carry a variety of dry, refrigerated or frozen food. Many food manufacturers, supermarkets and large food retailers buy directly from foreign suppliers.

A large number of multinational companies have established themselves in the region by entering one of the MERCOSUR countries and then developing the logistical and distribution systems required to enter other markets in the trading bloc. While the Brazilian market is large, diverse and difficult to penetrate and serve, Brazil's geographical position makes it an ideal entry country. The South-eastern region, which includes the states of Rio de Janeiro and São Paulo, is the most attractive regional test market.

Brazilian retailers have built up good relationships with local and foreign suppliers, and have put increasing emphasis on developing their own brands and engaging in relationship marketing. Most of the food sold by small independent stores has traditionally been distributed by wholesalers. The wholesale sector has developed considerably over the last 40 years, and as well as making regular deliveries wholesalers extend credit and offer rebates. Some large wholesalers have moved into retailing, thus adopting a strategy of vertical integration to counter the growing market pressures. Brazilian retailers also use importers who specialize in a particular product, such as nuts, meat products or fruit. These importers account for more than a third of food imports and have developed good relationships with super- and hypermarket chains, convenience stores and non-specialized wholesalers.

Although the large investments made recently in the supermarket sector have not yet paid off, there has been a slow revival of business, reflecting the positive trends in the economy as a whole. The Brazilian Supermarket Association predicts that supermarket sales will increase in 2005–7.

As discussed earlier, class A and B consumers mostly shop in large supermarkets, particularly those owned by the top five chains, while class D and E consumers do the bulk of their food shopping in small supermarkets, traditional grocery stores and street markets as the prices charged by the large retailers are mostly beyond their means. 'Mom and pop' stores are very popular with low-income consumers and in 2000 there were 270 000 such outlets. They mostly sell locally produced goods, with the exception of snacks. There is a strong presence of domestic companies in convenience store retailing, the most important of which are AMPM, BR Mania, Hungry Tiger, Select, and Stop and Shop. The recent trends in market share are shown in Figure 3.10.

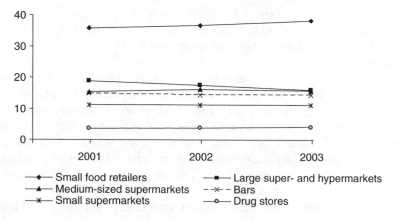

Figure 3.10   Share of food retail revenue, by type of outlet, Brazil, 2001–3 (per cent)
Source: ACNielsen Retail Indices.

All significant retailers have introduced e-commerce in both the business-to-business and the business-to-consumer market. The internet is being used to source new products and increase market penetration. Companies are eager to distinguish their product range and offers from those of direct competitors and give Brazilians better value for money. In general the internet has increased transparency in the retail market.

Promotion

A constitutional amendment made in 2002 permits foreign investment of up to 30 per cent in the well-developed Brazilian media market. The country ranks seventh in the world in terms of advertising expenditure, with more than US$7 billion spent in 2002. This ranking conceals large differences between expenditure in Brazil and that in the USA, Japan, UK, Germany, France, and Italy. For example Brazil spends only about 3 per cent of the total advertising expenditure in the United States, 30 per cent of that in Germany and 12 per cent of that in Japan. However in terms of advertising expenditure as a share of GDP, in Brazil the share of about 1 per cent is on a par with that in Japan and the United Kingdom and more than that in Germany, France and Italy. Total expenditure for the period 1995–2002 is shown in Figure 3.11.

The economic and investment downturn at the beginning of the twenty-first century drove the promotion industry into a serious crisis.

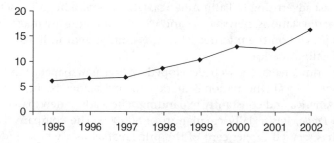

Figure 3.11 Advertising expenditure, Brazil, 1995–2002 (billion Brazilian reals)
Source: Projeto Intermeios.

By mid 2004 the total credit extended to media corporations reached US$3.3 billion due to huge investments in cable television that have not resulted in any return.

In 2001 the media in Brazil consisted of five TV stations, more than 120 cable and satellite channels, 3000 radio stations, more than 2000 regional and local newspapers (a quarter of which were dailies), 1500 magazines and about 42 000 billboards. One hundred and fifty million people watched television commercials and more than 160 million listened to radio advertisements on a daily basis. Advertising expenditure varied by media type (Table 3.4).

The main advertising medium in Brazil is television, but since 1992 there has been a downward trend in the share of TV advertising in overall advertising expenditure. This is mostly due to the high degree of frag-mentation in TV viewing and the large number of viewers who watch cable and satellite broadcasts. The TV giant Globo Holdings, known as Platinum Venus, has 60 per cent of the TV audience and 80 per cent of

Table 3.4 Share of Brazilian media in advertising expenditure, 1997 and 2001 (per cent)

	1997	2001
Television	59.0	57.3
Newspapers	24.0	21.2
Magazines	9.0	10.6
Radio	5.0	4.7
Outdoor media	3.0	6.2

Source: Projeto Intermeios.

broadcast advertising in Latin America. Globo owns a huge TV network, many radio stations, newspapers and weekly and monthly magazines. It is also present on the internet. Thus it is omnipresent in Brazil and the rest of Latin America.

The print media are well developed. While newspapers tend to be regional or local, the national market for magazines is the largest in Latin America and constantly expanding. The leading newspaper, *Folha de São Paulo*, has a daily circulation of 800000. The company Editora Abril has secured 75 per cent of the print market as a whole and more than 90 per cent of the magazine market. The most successful magazine, *Veja*, has a circulation of 1.2 million, among the largest in the world. There are several other magazines with a high circulation and countrywide appeal, including *Exame, Isto E, Senhor* and *Visão*.

Urban Brazilians spend about 35 hours a week listening to radio broadcasts, 18 hours watching television and 10 hours reading newspapers or magazines. Almost all watch television, about two thirds listen to radio programs and more than a half read newspapers or magazines. TV Globo is preferred by four fifths of television viewers. FM radio stations such as BH, Cidade and Guarani attract larger audiences than AM stations. Brazilians almost exclusively read newspapers from their own region. The content and format of regional dailies are similar to those of the *The New York Times* and *The Washington Post*.

The internet is popular with youngsters in the large urban centers and with employed, highly skilled specialists. More than 23 million people (about 12.5 per cent of the population) surf the internet.

While companies of all sizes and ownership structure engage in promotion, small companies spend very little on it and mainly use low-profile outdoor media, brochures and newspapers. The bulk of advertising expenditure is generated by a small number of large companies. The top spenders are Casas Bahia, Grupo Silvio Santos, Unilever Brazil, Companhia Brasileira de Distribuição, Volkswagen/Seat, Fiat, Telefónica, General Motors, Telecom Italia and the government of Brazil, which accounted for more than a third of expenditure in 2003.

Conclusion

Brazil is among the most attractive emerging markets in the world, with a large market potential and a diverse economy. Due to its abundant natural resources, large demand base and high degree of market liberalization it was the recipient of huge amounts of foreign investment in the second half of the 1990s. The gradual economic revival has laid the foundations for the continuous growth of business-to-business and business-to-consumer markets. The growing international competitiveness of the economy has boosted exports, thus improving the trade balance and stimulating a flow of outward investment.

The strong position of the steel-making, automotive, food-processing and aircraft industries is supplemented by the well-developed agricultural sector and the rapidly growing service sector.

The domestic market has undergone significant changes, with an increased number of smaller households, a larger number of employed women and a general decline in the income of class C and D consumers. Consumption patterns have also changed. Brazilians show a growing preference for ready-made or easy to prepare food and reasonably priced consumer goods of high quality and improved performance. Although consumers have been exhibiting higher price sensitivity since the mid 1990s, more affluent consumers can still be tempted to buy new products and willingly make trial purchases.

Because Brazilians are highly attracted to well-known brands, these account for a large proportion of household expenditure. However the low purchasing power of the majority of the population has encouraged the creation of so-called B brands. The market share of these is constantly rising, thus threatening the position of mighty global brands such as Kellogg and Nestlé.

The increased inflow of FDI has intensified domestic competition and put immense pressure on local companies to improve their performance and competitiveness.

Recommended reading

Baer, W. (2001) *The Brazilian Economy: Growth and Development* (Westport, CT: Praeger).

Beausang, F. (2003) *Third World Multinationals: Engine of Competitiveness or New Form of Dependency?* (Basingstoke: Palgrave Macmillan).

Font, M. (2002) *Brazil: Development, Industrialization, and Social Transformation* (Lanham, MD: Rowman & Littlefield).

Hurrell, A. and L. Pinheiro (eds) (2003) *Brazil in the World: Globalization and State Power* (London: I. B. Tauris).

Oliveira, J. (2001) *Brazil: A Guide for Business People* (Yarmouth, ME: Intercultural Press).

Ribeiro, D. (2001) *The Brazilian People: The Formation and Meaning of Brazil* (Tampa, FA: University Press of Florida).

4
Marketing in Chile

Map 3   Chile
Source: www.joeskitchen.com/chile/facts/map.htm.

Brief historical background

Historical evidence suggests that the first inhabitants of what is now Chile date back some 10000 years. These were migrating Indian tribes who settled in the Andean valleys and along the coast of the Southern Pacific Ocean. The Inca Empire gradually extended its territory to northern Chile and the dominant Indian group, the Araucanians, fell subject to the Incas.

Spanish colonization began after Diego de Almagro was sent by Francisco Pizarro to capture the south-west region of South America, including the central lowlands of Chile. De Almagro's successor, Pedro de Valdivia, subdued the Araucanians, occupied Chile and founded the settlements of Santiago, La Serena, Concepción and Valdivia. Gaining full control of the region involved continuous warfare with the native population.

Initially the Spanish colonizers found Chile unattractive because of its historical separation from its northern neighbor, Peru. At that time Chile's natural resources had yet to be discovered, so large ranches and haciendas were established and indigenous people were put to work. Most of the produce was shipped to Peru. The mestizos became tenant farmers and were classed as *inquilinos*. Although legally free, in practice the *inquilinos* were tied to the land.

For a long time the colony was ruled by the viceroy of Peru. In 1778 it became independent from Peru but remained a Spanish colony. As most of the boundaries of the colonies were not precisely set, Chile was embroiled in continuous territorial disputes and conflicts with neighboring Peru, Bolivia and Argentina.

A movement for Chilean independence began in 1810, led by Juan Martínez de Rozas and Bernardo O'Higgins. Lack of unity among the liberation fighters resulted in a series of defeats, but in 1817 General José de San Martín led an army across the Andes from Argentina to Chile, and in 1818 he defeated the Spaniards at the battle of Maipú.

Chile's independence was declared on 12 February 1818. O'Higgins became the supreme director of Chile and ruled the country for the next five years. Under the command of Lord Cochrane of Britain the Chilean navy cleared the coastline of Spanish ships. In 1823 the military and some members of the newly born Chilean intelligentsia formed a government with the intention of introducing radical democratic reforms. The constitution of 1833 marked the establishment of parliamentary democracy and the start of a long period of political stability.

The period 1840–60 was characterized by governmental reforms and economic advancement. After war with Bolivia and Peru in 1879–83, Chile annexed the nitrate fields in the Atacama desert region, which previously had been laid claim to by Bolivia. Chile also had serious territorial disputes with Argentina, but these did not lead to military confrontation.

Prospecting for minerals continued and attracted the interest of US investors. Substantial deposits of nitrate and copper were discovered, attracting more US capital for investment in mines. The amount of US capital invested in Chile grew to such an extent that the United States became a major financial player in the economic development of the country. Due to the growth of domestic businesses and the presence of powerful US interests the first 20 years of the twentieth century were a time of rapid infrastructural and industrial development. However widespread poverty and the foreign ownership of natural resources caused political instability and dictatorship was replaced by short-lived democratic governments. With the stabilization of the world economy after the First World War Chile's economic performance improved, but then the Great Depression had a negative impact on the country thanks to its reliance on mineral exports.

Industrialization gave rise to a sizable working class and powerful trade unions, which strengthened the influence of Marxism. Social harmony was disrupted by clashes between radicals and conservatives when the latter suppressed the struggle for social justice led by the former. The 1938 elections were won by a democratic, proreformist coalition that boosted economic activities. After the Second World War, in which Chile supported the Allies, successive governments introduced measures to improve labor conditions and curb the influence of communists. Social instability and political tension caused recurring labor crises and chronic inflation in the 1950s and early 1960s.

In the mid-1960s the government implemented land reforms and made improvements in education, housing and labor conditions. It also obtained controlling interests in US-owned copper mines, but it continued to rely on Americans to manage the mines. In 1970 Salvador Allende Gossens was sworn in as president of Chile, thus becoming the first Marxist president in Latin America. His aim was to turn Chile into a socialist people's state by nationalizing private companies, implementing land reforms and entering into economic and political cooperation with communist countries. Included in the nationalization program were the US-owned copper mines, which accounted for more than 83 per cent of Chile's export income. Nationalization also encompassed other foreign firms, oligopolistic industries, banks and large estates. Naturally these policies provoked hostility among foreign investors, and especially the US companies that had poured a lot of money into local business development.

Economic hardship and opposition to Allende's policies led to a series of violent strikes and demonstrations. Meanwhile the military put pressure on Allende to restrict his reformist aspirations, which resulted in the inclusion of some military representatives in the government. As US interests had been damaged the US administration set out to destabilize Chile by exerting strong economic pressure and using opposition political groups and the media to encourage a military coup. In September 1973 the armed forces, led by General Augusto Pinochet Ugarte, staged a coup. Allende and many thousands of his supporters were killed, detained or expelled from the country. The economic downturn continued after the overthrow of Allende, despite the immediate implementation of a denationalization policy (government ownership of key enterprises was preserved). Pinochet proclaimed himself undisputed head of state and in 1977 abolished all political parties and restricted human and civil rights. In the late 1970s and early 1980s, with the help of foreign bank loans the economy began to stabilize but unemployment was on the rise, labor unrest increased, foreign debt grew and the country was plunged into recession.

Under the pressure of growing internal discontent Pinochet allowed some democratic changes to be made in the constitution of 1981. The 1980s marked the beginning of political reforms, despite the continuation of military dictatorship. In 1989 Patricio Aylwin Azócar was elected president but Pinochet preserved some of his power as he remained head of the army. The Aylwin government introduced some democratic reforms, the economy was strengthened and exports increased, thus reducing Chile's foreign debt. Aylwin's successor, Eduardo Frei Ruiz-Tagle, implemented free-market reforms that led to a massive inflow of FDI and rapid economic growth. However in the late 1990s falling copper prices and the Asian economic crisis resulted in the return of economic and social problems.

In January 2000 Ricardo Lagos Escobar became president and set about finding ways to fight unemployment and resolve the ongoing political tension with Bolivia over the latter's demand for access to the Pacific Ocean via the land annexed by Chile in the 1800s. Lagos's presidency has benefited from his internationally acknowledged political, legal and economic capabilities, and he has created new opportunities for the growth of foreign trade within the framework of newly signed free trade agreements with the United States, the European Union and South Korea. Numerous reforms have been undertaken, encompassing infra-structural projects and social improvement programs.

Economic overview

Chile is considered to have the most stable economy in Latin America. About 80 per cent of the 625 000 or so companies are private, many with foreign capital investment. More than 99 per cent of companies are small and medium-sized, but for many years large corporations have generated over 50 per cent of GDP.

In 1989–98 the economy grew at an impressive rate, but the Asian crisis and the subsequent global economic slowdown caused a moderate recession. GDP grew by 4.5 per cent in 2000, 3.4 per cent in 2001, 2.2 per cent in 2002 and 3.3 per cent in 2003 (Figures 4.1 and 4.2). It is esti-mated that GDP will grow at about 5–6 per cent per annum in 2005–8. Per capita GDP has followed the general trend of GDP, with stagnation in 2001–2, a slight increase in 2003 and a more substantial rise in 2004 (Figure 4.3). The buoyant economy has also had a positive effect on the domestic savings and investment rates, which have increased substantially.

Since 1973 Chile has encouraged private business growth and foreign direct investment. Immediately after the coup by Pinochet the trade blockade on the country was lifted and loans were extended by the US government and international financial institutions to help overcome

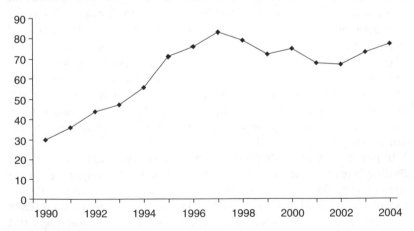

Figure 4.1   GDP, Chile, 1990–2004 (US$ billion)
Source: www.dbresearch.com.

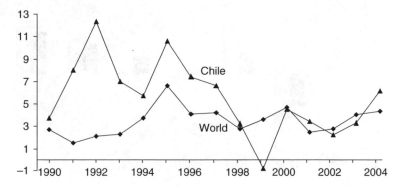

Figure 4.2 Average GDP growth, Chile and the world, 1990–2004 (per cent)
Source: www.dbresearch.com, Trade Chile.

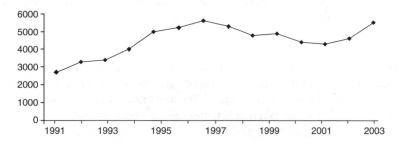

Figure 4.3 Per capita GDP, Chile, 1990–2004 (US dollars)
Source: www.dbresearch.com.

the country's severe financial difficulties. Chile has pursued generally sound economic policies for nearly three decades. The 1973–90 military government returned many state-owned companies to their previous owners and privatized others. Since 1990 the three democratic governments have implemented market reforms, liberalized the economy and slowed down the privatization process. Private capital investment in domestic companies and the financial sector is welcomed and there has been a considerable inflow. The government has almost no involvement in the economy, apart from its regulatory role and its control of a number of large companies, such as the copper giant CODELCO.

In the last few years unemployment has stabilized at 8–10 per cent, well above the average of 5 per cent in the 1990s. Living standards have improved markedly since the 1980s. The proportion of Chileans living below the poverty line fell from 46 per cent of the population in 1987

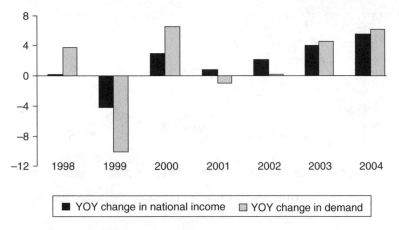

Figure 4.4   Year-on-year change in national income and consumer demand (per cent), Chile, 1998–2004
Source: Trade Chile.

to 18.8 per cent in 2003. Due to productivity improvements, on average wages have risen faster than the rate of inflation and disposable income has risen too. This is also partly due to the low inflation rate. The independent Central Bank has taken strict measures to keep annual inflation in the range of 2–4 per cent, and it has not exceeded 5 per cent since the late 1990s. In 2003 it was as low as 1.1 per cent.

The relative stability and low risk of the Chilean economy were not enough to boost consumer demand in the first two years of the twenty-first century following the severe fall of national income in 1998 and 1999, but it slowly recovered in 2003 and 2004 (Figure 4.4).

Foreign trade

The Chilean economy is highly dependent on foreign trade. The present government has applied a consistent policy of export promotion and free trade expansion. A large proportion of GDP has traditionally been generated from exports. In 2003 their contribution amounted to 29 per cent, having risen constantly since 1994. In 1994 the ratio of foreign trade to GDP was less that 52 per cent but by 2003 it had risen to 69 per cent. In 1991–2000 exports increased by 131 per cent and imports by 78 per cent. Between 1999 and 2003 the value of exports consistently exceeded that of imports, and in 2003 the trade surplus amounted to US$3.3 billion (Figure 4.5).

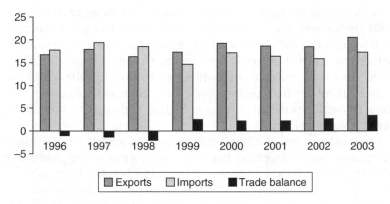

Figure 4.5   Foreign trade, Chile, 1996–2003 (US$ billion)
Source: Banco Central de Chile.

Copper accounts for a sizable proportion of exports, and the state-owned firm CODELCO is the largest copper producer in the world. Copper and other exports have experienced steady growth since the mid-1970s. In the early 1970s the share of non-mineral exports in total exports was about 30 per cent, but by 2003 they accounted for more than 60 per cent. The major non-mineral exports are fruit, processed food, fish, shellfish, wine, timber and wood products. About 22 per cent of exports go to the United States, Chile's largest export market. European countries absorb about 25 per cent of the value of total export, Asia more than 33 per cent and Latin America about 17 per cent. Exports to Asia have experienced the fastest growth since 1999. Exports to that part of the world include unrefined copper, copper products, manufactured goods, fruit and wine. In 2000 the top 5 exports destinations were the United States, Japan, the United Kingdom, Brazil, and China, accounting for about half of the value of Chilean export.

With regard to imports, economic growth and growth in domestic consumer demand have triggered an increase and imports amounted to US$17.9 billion in 2003. Imports are dominated by industrial products. In 2003 technology and capital equipment comprised about 21 per cent of total imports and the share of industrial goods in the total value of imports was 78 per cent in 2002. In 2000–2 imports came mostly from the United States, Argentina, Brazil, China and Japan. In 2000 about 20 per cent of imports came from the United States, but its share had declined to 13.6 per cent by 2003. In that year Argentina took the lead with more than 20 per cent, followed by the European Union with about 17 per cent.

In its attempt to encourage imports from a wide range of countries, in 2003 the government lowered the import tariffs charged to countries with which Chile did not have a trade agreement, and it has consistently reduced tariffs by 1 per cent per annum. Currently most imports are subject to a small universal tariff, while imports from Canada and Mexico, Chile's current free trade partners, are exempt from all tariffs. Nevertheless some protectionist measures remain, such as higher tariffs on imported sugar, wheat and flour.

The participation of Chile in bilateral and multilateral economic agreements and trading blocs has been instrumental in the growth of its international trade. The intention is to make Chile the Latin American country with greatest access to leading world markets because the small domestic market cannot support sustained economic growth. In 1993 Chile signed economic cooperation agreements with Bolivia, Venezuela and Colombia, and in 1994 with Ecuador. Among the many free trade agreements are those with Canada, Mexico, the United States, the European Union and Central America, which facilitate cross-border movements of goods and services as well as providing opportunities for increased investment and bilateral cooperation. Chile is also an associate member of MERCOSUR, and is one of the few countries to sign an economic cooperation agreement with Cuba. Moreover it joined the Asia-Pacific Economic Cooperation Forum (APEC) in 1993, and in 2002 it finalized a free trade agreement with South Korea. It also has preferential trade agreements with Venezuela, Colombia and Ecuador, and strongly supports the idea of Latin American integration and a free trade area throughout the Americas.

Foreign direct investment

Foreign direct investment (FDI) is regulated centrally by the government's Foreign Investment Committee. Encouragement of foreign investment is laid down in the constitution, and since the mid-1970s FDI has been an essential part of Chile's national development strategy, based on market orientation, liberalization and internationalization of the economy.

FDI has declined since the extraordinary boom in the late 1990s, falling from just over US$9.6 billion in 1999 to US$2.9 billion in 2004 (Figure 4.6). The factors that accounted for this downturn were the overall fall in global FDI between 2000 and 2003, economic instability in other Latin American countries and the divergence of FDI to the Far East. Nevertheless the Chilean economy did not plunge into crisis. The government has since been active in promoting the country as an

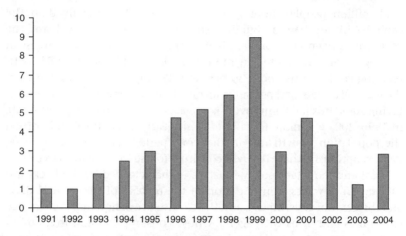

Figure 4.6   Inward foreign direct investment, Chile, 1991–2004 (US$ billion)
Source: Foreign Investment Committee.

investment platform for foreign companies and multinational corporations wishing to invest in the region or expand their operations in Latin
America. The inflow of FDI has recently fallen due to the greater use of
local capital markets by foreign investors, encouraged by the high
liquidity and dynamism of the financial system and its consistently low
interest rates. The liberal foreign investment regime is reflected in
the Foreign Investment Law, which provides foreign investors with the
same rights as Chilean investors. Foreign investors can freely use the
official foreign exchange market to repatriate their profits and capital.

Between 1974 and 2003 cumulative FDI rose to US$64.4 billion, more
than two thirds in the mining industry. Two thirds of the total came
from North America and Spain. Currently more than 3000 international
companies from at least 60 countries have operations in Chile.

According to the Foreign Investment Committee, FDI more than doubled between 2003 and 2004. Most of this went into energy generation,
transportation, telecommunications and mining. Spain accounted for
more than 80 per cent of FDI in 2004, 75 per cent of which came from
the Spanish energy company Endesa España and the mobile telephone
company Telefónica Moviles.

Market characteristics

The Chilean market has the greatest potential in Latin America. According
to the National Institute of Statistics, in 2003 the population amounted

15.2 million people, more than 40 per cent of whom lived in the capital. Chileans have a high life expectancy and literacy level, and the economy is open and comparatively stable. GDP is the sixth largest in the region and amounted to more than US$72 billion in 2003, with retailing contributing about 30 per cent. Per capita GDP is higher than the regional average and per capita income is second only to that in Mexico. Living standards have improved as the average annual GDP growth rate in 1996–2004 was more than 3 per cent, nearly three times higher than the population growth rate in the same period. The Chilean Central Bank is optimistic that GDP will continue to rise in the coming years.

Fiscal and monetary policy in Chile is characterized by the backward indexation of wages, consolidation of the policies of the Central Bank and the Chilean government, and the coexistence of liquidity-constrained consumers and firms with agents whose consumption and investment decisions are not constrained by government policy (Schmidt-Hebbel and Serven, 1995). This enables a high degree of flexibility when making permanent or temporary fiscal and monetary changes, and when responding to unanticipated developments. Moreover inflation has been kept low (1.1 per cent in 2003) and the Chilean peso is stable *vis-à-vis* major currencies such as the US dollar and the euro.

Chile is used by foreign companies as a lead market to penetrate Latin America. For example the US manufacturer Ingersol-Rand opened a trade center in Chile in 2002 to target the other markets in the region. Similarly the German mining and infrastructure subcontractor Thyssen Group set up trading and contracting operations to serve as a stepping stone to the rest of Latin America. Essential to a company's success in any foreign country are knowledge of the local market, strategic approaches and tactical adaptations that are tailored to that market. In the case of Chile, partnerships with highly experienced domestic companies with local marketing expertise are more suitable than any other form of FDI.

Consumer behavior

Chileans have a collectivist culture, strong family ties and high uncertainty avoidance (Hofstede, 2001). This affects purchasing behavior in respect of both everyday and occasional shopping.

The consumption patterns for food and beverages have been consistent over the past 15 years. About a fifth of household income is spent on food and beverages. In the case of the latter the biggest sellers are soft drinks, wine and milk. The greatest volume of milk is bought by class

A and B consumers, and the greatest volume of soft drinks is purchased by consumers in classes C and D. Detergents also account for a significant proportion of household spending. In 2003 the average monthly household expenditure on food and beverages was US$139 for class A and B consumers, about US$110 for class C consumers and less than US$80 for class D consumers.

Chileans are conservative shoppers and normally buy the same grocery products every week. A small percentage of class A and B consumers occasionally try new products but they do not spend much on impulse or trial purchases.

Urban consumers mostly shop in supermarkets, traditional stores, pharmacies and perfumeries. Open markets are frequented by about 33 per cent of urban shoppers, compared with more than 90 per cent of consumers in rural areas.

Seventy five per cent of Chilean households, mostly urban consumers, purchase their food supplies once a week. Only about 10 per cent of their food budget is spent on week days, and weekend shopping peaks on Saturdays. While this buying pattern is typical for all Chileans, it is especially so for classes C, D and E consumers. About 66 per cent of households prefer family shopping and about 75 per cent of individuals opt to shop with friends or relatives.

Promotion does not have a significant impact on purchasing decisions of Chileans. Based on the findings of a number of consumer surveys, only about 11 per cent of total household expenditure is spent on purchases influenced by advertisements or other promotional activities. Planned shopping expenditure accounts for 80 per cent of total household spending. Chilean consumers are highly price sensitivite and are considerably more responsive to permanent price reductions than to temporary sales. This is especially the case with everyday goods with high consumption rates.

Chileans have a more positive attitude towards national than towards foreign brands. Therefore, foreign brands find it difficult to appeal to consumers and charge premium prices. The overwhelming perception is that most foreign brands are not worth their high prices and that local brands are of better quality and offer the right value and benefits. The only brands that are recognized for their brand premium are top global brands such as Rolex, Gucci, Montblanc and Omega. Younger people from classes A and B are most attracted to foreign branded goods.

A number of studies have compared the buying behavior of Chilean consumers with that of consumers in other countries. For example Nicholls *et al.* (2000) and Li *et al.* (2003) have compared Chilean consumer behavior with that of US and Chinese consumers respectively. Most Chilean and Chinese consumers visit shopping malls with the sole intention of making purchases, whereas a high percentage of US consumers go to malls only to look around. With regard to preferences for specific outlets, Chilean and Chinese consumers give first and second priority to the merchandise offered and the atmosphere in the store respectively. Their third priority is store location. The same criteria are important to US buyers, but in a different order. They put store atmosphere first, location second and merchandise third.

Chileans are quickest of the three nations' shoppers and the majority spend less than half an hour in shopping malls. Most Chinese spend an hour, and Americans spend at least three hours, sometimes without buying anything. Chileans shop in a restricted number of outlets and have a high degree of loyalty to particular outlets. They prefer to do all their food and non-food shopping in a single visit to a chosen mall. Moreover many combine shopping with eating out and socializing, mostly during late Saturday afternoon or at night.

Chilean consumers tend to be utilitarian, rational and unhedonistic. This makes them difficult to influence so marketers have to emphasize rationality in the design and implementation of their campaigns. As most consumers only buy what they have planned in advance, information on the availability and features of products must be conveyed to them beforehand. Such an approach becomes even more appropriate when considering the fact that at least eight out of ten consumers finalize their purchases in less than half an hour during which their attention is mostly preoccupied with the execution of planned purchases thus leaving extremely limited time for marketers to influence buying behavior in the store premises.

Since 2001 the consumption of snacks, cereals, pet food, deodorants and canned fish has been on the rise. That of coffee, dairy cream and mayonnaise has reduced, which has brought down their prices. The lower prices have not counteracted the falling sales revenues, although there has been a slight increase in the volume of sales.

Retailing

Bianchi and Mena (2004) have studied the dynamics of the retail sector in Chile. Their findings show that Chilean retailers have become highly conscious of the need to protect their operations against foreign market entrants. The largest grocery, home improvement and department stores are owned by Chilean family business groups (Table 4.1) that are

Table 4.1 Principal retail chains, Chile, 2002

	Market share (%)	Number of stores
Department stores		
Falabella	21.5	31
Ripley	10.0	31
Almacenes Paris	9.5	16
Grocery retailers		
D&S	30.0	62
Santa Isabel	9.7	76
Jumbo	8.5	7
Home improvement retailers		
Sotimac	16.3	49
HomeStore	3.3	7
Easy	2.3	15
Pharmaceutical retailers		
FASA	33.0	234
SalcoBrand	33.0	230
Cruz Verde	28.0	290

Source: ACNielsen (2002); Bianchi and Mena (2004).

seeking to retain and possibly increase their market share through new product introduction and market development strategies.

As the national market is relatively small the competition between domestic players is fierce, but they are united in opposing the entry of foreign rivals and therefore large international retailers have found it difficult to establish operations in Chile. Some global retailers, such as Sears, tried but incurred huge losses and consequently withdrew, while the mighty Wal-Mart developed operations in neighboring markets but did not attempt to set foot in Chile. Domestic retailers have promoted growth through consolidation and imitation of the best practices of global retailers. This, together with their strong local market knowledge and expertise and Chilean consumers' highly conservative shopping habits and reservations about foreign brands, have created high market entry barriers against foreign retailers in the otherwise liberalized Chilean marketplace.

The highly competitive retail industry has two new entrants: Quienco and Consorcio, which bought ownership stakes in the country's third-largest retailer, Almacenes Paris. The share price of the latter rose by more than a third after the Gálmez family, who had controlled the company for more than 100 years, sold their controlling 52.4 per cent stake on a flotation making the ownership of Almacenes Paris dispersed.

In August 2003 Falabella, the leading department store chain, merged with Sodimac, the top purveyor of home appliances and construction materials. In the same month Cencosud acquired two supermarket chains: Santa Isabel (purchased from Ahold of the Netherlands) and Agas. Then in December 2003 the market leader in supermarkets, D&S, prevented Falabella from entering the supermarket business by outbidding it by US$124 million in a competition to acquire Carrefour Chile, the French chain's Chilean operation. After the acquisition D&S applied Wal-Mart's 'low prices every day' strategy, thus setting off a price war in the whole retail industry.

Between 1999 and 2003 there was an average 1.2 per cent annual increase in the number of retail outlets in Chile, which was equal to the population growth rate during that period. In 2003 the total number of retail outlets was estimated at 107 000. As some regional supermarket chains have closed down, traditional stores, mini self-service supermarkets and kiosks mostly account for the rise in the number of outlets. The number of pharmacies and perfumeries has been on the increase since 2001, and currently they account for 12 per cent of outlets. Supermarkets still have the largest share of outlets (Figure 4.7).

With the concentration and improved efficiency of the large retail chains due to technological innovation, service improvement and greater financial provision, smaller shops have been put under severe pressure. The share of supermarket sales in GDP in 2002 was 6.6 per cent. In 1957 D&S was the first supermarket to open in Chile, and it still

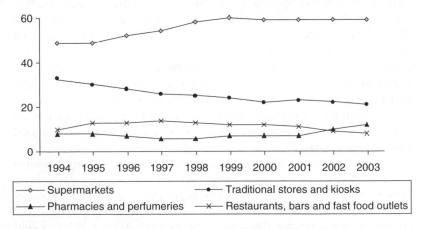

Figure 4.7 Share of total retail outlets, Chile, 1994–2003 (per cent)
Source: Censo ACNielsen Chile 2003; Arica a P. Montt y P. Arenas.

maintains a strong position today. D&S and Cencosud have been the leaders in developing store brands and retail formats such as discount supermarkets and hypermarkets, which benefit from integrated logistics and discount prices. D&S has three store brands: Lider, Econo and Almac, of which Lider is the most competitive. Cencosud is the owner of Jumbo, a hypermarket chain that offers a wide choice and excellent service. It was the first hypermarket to open in Chile and mostly targets class A and B consumers. Cencosud became the second largest player in Chilean retailing with the acquisition of Santa Isabel. Falabella, founded in 1889, has a diverse product and service offering and presently is the undisputed department store leader.

The openness of the economy encourages foreign trade and the balanced structure of exports and imports has been essential in improving the competitiveness of the Chilean retail market. However the aggressive competition has affected profit margins, forcing retailers to adopt proactive and resourceful approaches to internationalization.

The largest Chilean retailers have entered other Latin American countries. For example Falabella is present in Argentina and Peru, Sodimac in Colombia, Ripley in Peru and Jumbo in Argentina. Thus the control Chilean retailers enjoy over the domestic market has enabled them to grow, expand into other markets in Latin America and avoid the threat posed by global retailers.

Advertising

The advertising industry in Chile has experienced problems and revenues have been falling since 1997 (Figure 4.8), although a slight revival took place in 2003. Domestic consumption, which is a major indicator of advertising expenditure, is still recovering from the impact of the

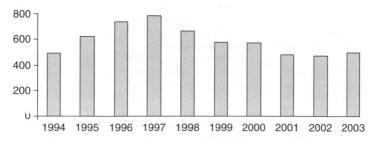

Figure 4.8 Advertising revenue, Chile, 1994–2003 (US$ million)
Source: Asociación Chilena de Agencias de Publicidad.

Asian crisis and the global economic slowdown. Another major reason for the decline in advertising expenditure is the general consolidation of all economic sectors, which has resulted in a fall in the amount of money industries are willing to spend on promotion. From 1999 advertising agencies themselves began to consolidate as a result of the falling demand for promotional activities.

The advertising industry in Chile is highly concentrated. Ten or so large advertisers are responsible for more than three quarters of total advertising expenditure. There are about 30 large advertising agencies, many of which are either subsidiaries or partners of multinational advertising corporations.

Chilean advertisers insist on originality and creative approaches to advertising campaigns as Chilean consumers have become highly demanding about the quality and originality of commercials. Some locally produced advertisements also have international appeal. An example of this is the Latin American advertisement for McDonald's Happy Meal brand. Global companies with operations in Chile have to create an even stronger local appeal if they are to achieve higher market shares or reposition existing brands.

The ten companies with the highest advertising expenditure account for two thirds of total expenditure (Table 4.2). About a third of this is spent by global companies with operations in Chile and the rest comes from Chilean and smaller international players.

Television is the preferred advertising medium for both advertisers and consumers, and it accounts for more than 50 per cent of advertising expenditure (Table 4.3). There are three major commercial channels:

Table 4.2 Companies with the highest advertising expenditure, Chile, 2003

	Sector	Percentage of total advertising expenditure
Unilever Chile	Consumer products	12.1
Nestlé Chile	Food products	8.0
Procter & Gamble Chile	Consumer products	6.9
Falabella	Department store chain	6.5
Telefónica CTC Chile	Telecommunications	6.1
Ripley	Department store chain	5.0
Almacenes Paris	Department store chain	4.9
ECUSA	Beverages	4.8
Laboratorio Maver	Pharmaceuticals	3.9
Coca Cola de Chile	Beverages	3.8

Source: Asociación Chilena de Agencias de Publicidad.

Table 4.3 Advertising expenditure by medium, Chile, 1997 and 2003 (per cent)

	1997	2003
Television, including cable	45	52
Newspapers	35	28
Radio	11	9
Magazines	5	4
Outdoor advertising	4	7

Source: Asociación Chilena de Agencias de Publicidad.

Televisión Nacional, Canal 13 and Megavisión. However Chileans are very suspicious of advertisements and therefore TV advertising cannot deliver the results sought by advertisers in terms of increased sales revenue and profitability. Advertisements have a very low recognition rate in comparison with those in Argentina and Brazil. Moreover the price per unit of TV advertising time is comparatively low as the bargaining power of TV advertisers is weak. Many companies are unwilling to spend a lot on advertising. Hence it is not only the advertising industry that is experiencing revenue difficulties but also commercial TV channels. Nevertheless the Chilean advertising industry aspires to become a regional center of excellence based on creativity, originality of design and production capabilities. To this end the industry has to attract clients from all over Latin America.

Print media account for about a third of advertising expenditure. Although newspaper and magazine readership is relatively low, advertisers believe that informative advertisements targeted at the mass market can increase sales. Advertisements aimed at affluent consumers are mostly for real estate, high-quality private schools and expensive goods such as automobiles.

Online advertising is a relatively new phenomenon. The internet penetration rate is one of the highest in Latin America, with about 1 300 000 internet users (or more than 9 per cent of the population) in 2004. While companies are positive about online advertising as they can assess its appeal more easily and it costs less, the impact it has had on consumer spending so far has been minuscule.

Their strict Catholicism and traditional values have made Chileans sensitive to the content of advertisements and they will not tolerate any that go beyond accepted social norms. Companies such as Benetton have had serious problems with their promotional campaigns as they have not been adapted to the Chilean context. The real issue for the country's advertising industry is whether and to what extent it should abide by the cultural values and norms or push the boundaries in an attempt to counterbalance the strong cultural and religious conservatism.

Conclusion

Chile has undergone considerable economic development and improved its international competitiveness. It was the first country in Latin America to liberalize its economy and implement market reforms. Moreover its low country risk and the openness of the economy have provided Chile with the highest market potential in Latin America. Moreover the liberal attitude towards foreign capital inflow has attracted a significant number of multinational corporations.

Chile's sustained economic growth has been combined with strong participation in world trade. There has been a continuous drive for internationalization by many domestic companies, mostly via exporting or investing in foreign operations.

The sound economic performance has had a positive effect on people's income and increased their purchasing power. However consumer demand has only undergone a small increase as economic uncertainty has encouraged larger individual and household savings. Added to this are the traditionalist buying patterns of the majority of the population. Brand awareness is high and there is a clear preference for domestically produced branded products. The purchasing patterns are difficult to change as they are based on deeply embedded cultural and religious values.

With the second largest per capita GDP and the highest per capita income in Latin America, Chile has the most homogeneous income and sociodemographic structure in the region. While the relatively high level of unemployment is adversely affecting the economy and consumer demand, the government has adopted policies to reduce unemployment and improve social security.

Chile is often used as lead market by international companies to expand into other countries in Latin America, due mainly to the country's remarkable achievement in free market development and to the highly demanding nature of domestic consumers.

Recommended reading

Beausang, F. (2003) *Third World Multinationals: Engine of Competitiveness or New Form of Dependency?* (Basingstake: Palgrave Macmillan).
Caistor, N. (1998) *Chile in Focus: A Guide to the People, Politics and Culture* (New York, NY: Interlink) Books.

Lederman, D. (2005) *The Political Economy of Protection: Theory and the Chilean Experience* (Stanford, CA: Stanford University Press).

Mesa-Lago, S. (2003) *Market, Socialist, and Mixed Economies: Comparative Policy and Performance – Chile, Cuba, and Costa Rica* (Baltimore, MD: Johns Hopkins University Press).

Silva, E. (1998) *The State and Capital in Chile: Business Elites, Technocrats, and Market Economics* (Boulder, CO: Westview Press).

Wellenius, B. (2002) *Closing the Gap in Access to Rural Communication: Chile 1995–2002* (Washington, DC: World Bank).

5

Marketing in Mexico

Map 4   Mexico
Source: www.cia.gov/cia/publications/factbook/geos/mx.html.

Brief historical background

Archaeological evidence suggests that the territory of contemporary Mexico has been inhabited for 22 000 years. The American continent developed on its own for many thousands of years, which explains the originality of its civilization. More than 5000 years ago the indigenous peoples of northern Mexico lived from hunting while those in the south engaged in agriculture.

Although many groups of people with ethnic and linguistic differences lived in the territory they were culturally homogeneous. They had a simple structure of government and were the first people on Earth to use a 365 day calendar. The ancient peoples of Mexico built pyramids, had similar traditions, and worshiped the same gods and goddesses.

From 2000 BC to 500 AD nomadic tribes settled in Mexico and made a major contribution to the arts and sciences. The classical period of Mexican history, 500–800 AD, was marked by mass urbanization and outstanding advances in architecture and the arts. The next period, 800–1521 AD, was characterized by military conquests.

The Aztec culture is the best known of all Mexican cultures. The Aztec Empire was huge and powerful when the Spanish *conquistadors* arrived at the beginning of the sixteenth century, but after a few years of resistance the Empire was conquered by the army of Hernán Cortés.

The colonial period started in 1521 and continued for three centuries. In 1551 the first university on the American mainland was opened in Mexico City. Gradually the European approaches to architecture, social life and governance spread throughout Mexico, but by the beginning of the nineteenth century the country had developed its own national identity, with strong roots in its ancient past, glorious middle ages and colonial period.

The modern period of Mexican history began with the War of Independence (1810–21). In 1821 the first independent government was established and in 1822 Agustín de Iturbide was crowned Emperor of Mexico. In 1824 the Mexican Congress adopted the first constitution and the country became a federal republic under the presidency of Guadalupe Victoria. The United Kingdom and the United States were among the first states to recognize Mexico's independence. In 1825–26 noble titles and slavery were abolished and democratic rule was introduced. In 1827 the first Mexican treaty of international trade was signed with Denmark. In 1836 the region of Texas declared its independence from Mexico, provoking a war between Mexico and the United States. The war ended in 1847 with Mexico's defeat and the loss of more than half of its territory, including present-day Arizona, California, New Mexico and Texas. In 1859 president Benito Juárez issued the Laws of Reform, which established the separation of the Church and the state. In 1862 France's imperialist ambitions spread to Mexico, and in 1864 the country became an empire under the rule of Prince Maximilian of Hapsburg. In 1867, following the withdrawal of French troops, Maximilian was captured and shot and the Mexican Republic was re-established.

In 1911 the Mexican president elect, Francisco Madero, was assassinated, marking the start of the Mexican Revolution and leading to the adoption in 1917 of a new constitution, the most democratic of its time.

Between 1918 and 1938 Mexico underwent significant political and social changes, ending in 1938 with the expropriation by President Lázaro Cárdenas of the oil companies to strengthen the national economy. Mexico participated in the Second World War as an ally of the United States. Immediately after the war it became a founding member of the United Nations and signed the Charter of San Francisco. At the initiative of Mexico, the Treaty of Tlatelolco was signed in 1967, the first treaty to prohibit nuclear weapons in the territory of Latin America.

Thanks to political stability and continuous socioeconomic development in the twentieth century the country was transformed from a principally agricultural economy to one of the 15 most powerful economies in the world. A number of developments had a large impact on the modernization and globalization of the Mexican economy. In 1986 Mexico became a member of the General Agreement on Tariffs and Trade (GATT, now the World Trade Organization) and became an active proponent of free trade for developing nations. In 1993 Mexico, the United States and Canada signed the North American Free Trade Agreement (NAFTA). These developments were accompanied by ambitious programs for structural reform, privatization, liberalization and deregulation.

Economic overview

Covering an area of 1 958 201 square kilometers, rich in natural resources, including crude oil and gas, and with a population of 105 million, Mexico is one of the most significant and attractive emerging markets in the world. Its official language is Spanish and around 80 per cent of the inhabitants are Roman Catholic. In 1968 Mexico became the first Latin American country to host the Olympic Games.

Economic analysts argue that the socioeconomic crisis that began in the late 1960s was due to presidential and governmental administrative changes. It affected the most vulnerable and numerous section of the population and was associated with changes in the political and social environment. The social unrest culminated in the student movement repudiating the brutal authoritarian political system.

The 1970s were a time of rapid economic development that became known as the 'Mexican miracle'. Sustainable macroeconomic growth and economic stability were achieved, inflation was similar to that in the United States and the fiscal deficit fluctuated between 1 per cent and 3 per cent of GDP. Being a major oil exporter the country benefited significantly from the oil price increases in 1973 and 1979. Encouraged by this, Mexico borrowed extensively against the anticipated profits from future oil sales. Meanwhile the country's monetary and fiscal policies were conservative and rigidly regulated. Unfortunately the rewards from economic growth were not shared equally by all and there was an increase in the poverty gap.

In the first half of the 1980s Mexico fell into a serious financial and economic crisis. The government was unable to repay its enormous foreign debt due to falling oil prices and increased interest rates on foreign credit. In 1982 it defaulted on the debt, and under the pressure of the huge fiscal deficit the peso was overvalued. This unhealthy economic situation resulted in a capital drain and the government started to borrow from international institutions and governments on a large scale. At the end of 1985 Mexico's prospect of economic stabilization and growth was still grim. Overproduction of oil worldwide caused a sharp drop in price, resulting in the depletion of the country's foreign currency reserves. In 1986 the fiscal deficit doubled to 15.9 per cent of GDP and inflation stood at 105.8 per cent.

Mexico was in obvious need of new policies to encourage non-oil exports and acquire foreign currency from international trade. Thus the Courage and Growth Plan was announced in 1986 to accelerate structural changes and lower the commercial barriers between Mexico and the rest of the world. In the same year the Baker Plan gave Mexico the opportunity to receive a substantial amount of foreign capital, renegotiate the debt repayment deadlines and revive the economy.

Thereafter Mexico was continuously engaged in restructuring and reorienting the economy from import substitution to the implementation of market mechanisms, liberalization and more substantial involvement in international business operations. This was facilitated by membership of GATT and the consequent reduction of import and export taxes and tariffs. GATT membership was followed by gradual deregulation of the economy in an attempt to help to the underdeveloped private sector. Despite these efforts, economic inertia caused the inflation rate to rise to 159.2 per cent in 1987, prompting a substantial increase in interest rates and damaging the credibility of and trust in Mexico's economic policies. In 1987 the government attempted to boost the economy by liberalizing foreign trade and significantly reducing the tariffs on most imported products. This was accompanied by large-scale privatization with local and foreign capital and the deregulation of industry. Nonethess the economy continued to stagnate and inflation and interest rates remained high. In a desperate effort to reverse the negative economic trend the government decided to impose the implemention of the Israeli model, under which employees would receive no salary increases and companies would freeze their prices. The government was also committed to lowering the public deficit and using the exchange rate to reduce inflation. While inflation did drop to 51.7 per cent in 1988 and financial crisis was avoided, the foreign currency reserves had been reduced by the attempt to support a fixed exchange rate. Consequently a 'sterilizing monetary policy' was introduced to restrict capital drain by replacing all outward bound US dollars with pesos.

In the first half of the 1990s there were some economic successes, mostly at the macroeconomic level. Inflation was kept under control, GDP grew continuously and the current account deficit was kept low. At the end of 1994 a devaluation of the peso served to strengthen the financial system, and restrictive financial measures stabilized the banking system and financial infrastructure. Membership of NAFTA also helped Mexico to improve its economic performance and competitive position. Tariffs on intra-NAFTA trade in agricultural products were immediately reduced by 50 per cent and Mexico abolished all export–import licenses and non-tariff barriers to trade with its NAFTA partners. Mexico's membership of NAFTA also facilitated investment flows and the transportation of goods.

In 1995 the United States and the International Monetary Fund (IMF) provided Mexico with emergency financial support of US$52 billion to stabilize the economy. This external aid was complemented by a governmental program to deal with the economy's financial and structural problems. The implications for companies were not straightforward as capital flow into private companies was still stagnant.

The economic recession of the mid 1990s was short and the precrisis economic indicators were re-established by the beginning of 1997. The country's economic performance was improved and stabilized as a result of sound macroeconomic policies, but the full potential of the economy was far from being realized. The annual growth of GDP stayed below 4 per cent, average income and productivity remained poor but the population growth rate was high. In 1994–98 Mexico's trade with its NAFTA partners tripled, and by 1999 the value of exports to NAFTA and other countries was more than the combined export value of all the other Latin American countries. Moreover Mexico had the highest economic growth rate in the region. The changes in GDP and domestic demand in 1990–2004 are illustrated in Figure 5.1.

In 1997–2000 the National Program of Financial Development was implemented. It focused on medium-term economic achievements rather than short-term goals and was intended to establish a strong platform for macroeconomic stabilization.

In the 1990s GDP growth was rigorous, inflation fell (Figure 5.2) and the current account deficit was in the medium range. This relative stability was barely affected by the economic slowdown in the United States in 2001–3, thanks to the government's sound macroeconomic policies. The country's growing participation in international trade has further improved its prospect of economic growth and there is expectation of increased foreign direct investment. Moreover its

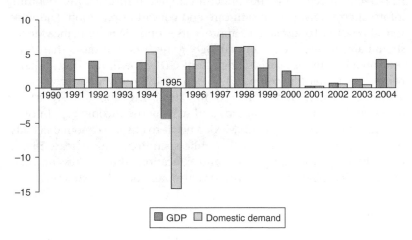

Figure 5.1 GDP and domestic demand, Mexico, 1990–2004 (per cent)
Sources: Instituto Nacional de Estadistica Geografía e Informácia; Mexican National Accounts; OECD Economic Outlook Database.

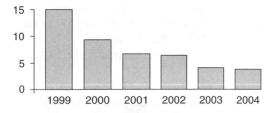

Figure 5.2 Annual inflation rate, Mexico, 1999–2004 (per cent)
Source: CIA World Factbook.

growing international competitiveness suggests that it can make significant economic progress through innovation and improved productivity. The continuous liberalization of the business environment and heightened market competition have increased the part played by market forces in regulating the economy. The objective of economic reforms is to preserve macroeconomic stability, further the implementation of market reforms, increase international competitiveness and improve living standards.

Mexico's efforts to improve business conditions and create a dynamic, attractive environment for local and foreign firms have been relatively successful. However there are still legal and regulatory restrictions that limit or prevent the flow of foreign capital into strategic economic sectors such as electricity generation. Moreover the GDP growth rate has been negatively affected by the underdeveloped infrastructure, booming informal economy, poor health-care and education provision, and widespread poverty. To sustain and improve its economic performance Mexico should aim to achieve an annual GDP growth rate of more than 6 per cent on a continuous basis. The present GDP growth rate of less than 4 per cent is rather low compared with the high population growth and low productivity, and it is too low to bring about a significant improvement in living standards and narrow the income gap. In order to achieve higher GDP growth Mexico needs to ensure economic stability, control taxation, corruption and public spending, and increase investment in infrastructural projects and education, thus addressing social problems and creating incentives for entrepreneurial investment.

Foreign trade

Mexico has continuously run a low trade deficit (Figure 5.3). In 2003 the deficit amounted to US$4.5 billion, with the value of exports at US$164.3 billion f.o.b. and that of imports at US$168.9 billion f.o.b. The United States is by far Mexico's largest trading partner, and in 2003 it accounted for 88 per cent of exports and 62 per cent of imports. Until 1994 the United States had a trade surplus in its bilateral trade with Mexico, but since 1995 it has been Mexico that has had a surplus (Figure 5.4). Other important destinations for Mexican exports are Canada and Germany.

Because of its membership in GAAT, the WTO and NAFTA, Mexico has made changes to its foreign trade policy and today it accounts for a large part of total Latin American foreign trade.

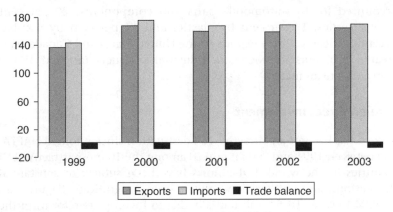

Figure 5.3   Foreign trade, Mexico, 1999–2003 (US$ billion)
Source: Deutsche Bank Research Country Infobase.

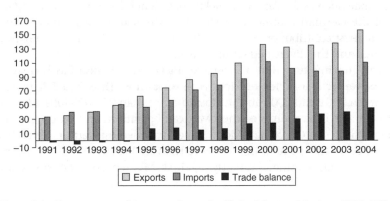

Figure 5.4   Exports to and imports from the United States, Mexico, 1991–2004
(US$ billion)
Source: US Census Bureau.

In the 1970s and 1980s oil and gas accounted for the bulk of Mexican exports, but by 2003 their share had dropped to little more than 11 per cent. Manufacturing has grown dramatically within the NAFTA setting, generating more than 85 per cent of export income in 2003. Approximately 50 per cent of manufactured exports are the product of assembly and procurement operations called *maquiladoras*, which were set up mostly with US and Canadian capital to produce consumer and industrial goods for re-export to the United States and Canada. About 40 per cent of the value of *maquiladora* exports is accounted for by automobile parts and components, 20 per cent by electronics, 17 per cent by plastics and 11 per cent by textiles. Recently, cheap Chinese exports to the United States and Canada have created problems for Mexican industrial products targeted at the North American market.

Foreign direct investment

Mexico has become an attractive FDI destination since it joined NAFTA, and between 1994 and 2003 it ranked among the 10 most attractive FDI countries in the world. FDI inflows have been subject to substantial fluctuations, and outflows have always been insignificant (Figure 5.5). In 2004 inward FDI fell substantially due to incomplete reforms in the telecommunication and energy sectors and a number of infrastructural problems. The largest foreign investments have come from multinationals such as the American Elektrisola, General Motors and Wal-Mart, and the German Daimler-Chrysler. The Mexican multinationals with the highest contribution to FDI outflow are Petróleos Méxicanos, PEMEX, Cemex and the diversified Grupo Carso.

The growing attraction of China as an FDI destination has had significant repercussions for Mexico, with an almost threefold fall in FDI between 2001 and 2003 and the loss of more than 250 000 jobs. Most of the firms that have divested their Mexican operations and set up production facilities in China have done so because medium-term profitability is expected to be much higher there than in Mexico. Other emerging markets that compete directly against Mexico for FDI flows are

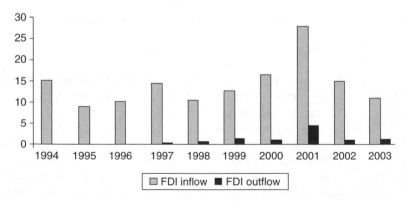

Figure 5.5   FDI inflows and outflows, Mexico, 1994–2003 (US$ billion)
Source: UNCTAD World Investment Report (2004).

India, Poland and Brazil. This competition is mostly for labor-intensive investments that are driven by efficiency seeking motives related to low-cost, large-scale production. It is difficult for Mexico to compete in this regard and therefore it should focus on higher value-added projects. However industrial and infrastructural development has not moved far enough to deal with such a challenge, so the government should instead provide institutional support for the development of knowledge-intensive industries. So far only the potential of the oil and gas industry has preserved the flow of capital from global foreign investors.

Despite the above, Mexico continues to benefit from FDI from its NAFTA partners. US companies rate the country as the fifth most attractive market in the world and Canadian investors rank it third.

Consumer behavior

There are more than 105 million consumers in Mexico and annual consumer expenditure is estimated at US$300 billion. More than 35 cities have a population of 500 000 or more. The growth in consumer spending is underpinned by growth in per capita GDP (Figure 5.6), growing household income and the low unemployment rate. Mexico has the highest per capita GDP in Latin America, although there are substantial income disparities and 40 per cent of people live below the poverty line.

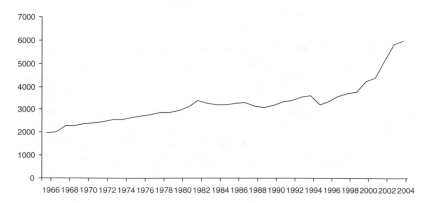

Figure 5.6   Per capita GDP, Mexico 1966–2004 (constant US dollars, 1995)
Source: World Development Indicators 2004, International Bank for Reconstruction and Development.

Research on consumer characteristics, including national identity, has shown that Mexicans score relatively highly on national heritage, cultural homogeneity and belief system, whereas consumer ethnocentrism is somewhat above average. These four characteristics make Mexican consumers rather similar to those in the United States (Keillor and Hult, 1999). Mexican society is typified by collectivism, high uncertainty avoidance, high power distance and a relatively strong masculine culture. People's sense of family is particularly strong and consumption is very much driven by family needs. Mexican consumers shop once or twice a week for themselves but several times a week for their children (Byrne, 1994). Bearing in mind that the average size of a Mexican family is 4.7 people and 40 per cent of households have more than six members, one can conclude that family-related spending is high for most people in Mexico. While the majority of consumers tend to search for the best value for money, those who can afford branded products are willing to switch to a different brand if they believe there is a good reason to do so (Turner, 2001). This has made Mexicans an attractive target for the producers of domestic and foreign (mostly US) branded goods.

In the case of fast moving consumer goods and consumer non-durables, Mexican consumers shop more frequently than their US and West European counterparts. They tend to buy food regularly during the week as the majority prefer fresh food and home-made meals. However there was a decline in the number of shopping trips per week from 11–12 in 1995 to 7–8 in 1999. Another factor that affects shopping frequency is that comparatively few people have a refrigerator. According to official statistics, many households cannot afford a refrigerator and if they can they are concerned about the cost of electricity. Moreover in 2000, 7 per cent of households (or 22 per cent of the population) did not have an electricity supply and 15 per cent had no running water.

Mexican consumers are very particular about the quality of food they eat. Most of them choose to buy fresh, additive-free food and express concern about the use of artificial ingredients and pesticides. Consequently there is a sizable market for health foods, which have an annual turnover of about US$600 million and attract more than six million customers, mostly high-income individuals aged 30–60 and living in large metropolitan areas. The most popular imported brands are Weight Watchers, Lean Cuisine and Healthy Choice, which are produced by global companies such as Nestlé, Kellogg and Quaker. They are sold in specialty stores, health-food chains and all major supermarkets.

Mexicans' taste preferences necessitate product customization. This has resulted in new products such as confectionery with chili, tortilla soup, and yoghurts and milk drinks flavored with exotic fruits such as mango and tamarind. Price sensitivity affects purchasing decisions, and consumers shop around to find the best quality food at the lowest possible price. In this regard open air markets and stalls that sell fresh fruit, vegetables and other food products are very popular. Mexican people have trust in the quality of locally produced food and enjoy good relationships with open-air vendors and small grocery retailers.

The greater diversity of food has created a new consumer group that is health oriented and looks mostly for low-carbohydrate products and fresh fruit and vegetables. The first of these are generally available only in supermarkets and are beyond the budget of all but high-income consumers. National statistics show that Mexican supermarket and chain store purchases are somewhat restricted by the low level of vehicle ownership. In 2002 there were 11.5 million registered motor vehicles, or about one vehicle per 10 people.

In 1999–2003 important economic changes took place in Mexico that had a substantial impact on consumer behavior. Low inflation brought about lower interest rates, which increased consumer confidence. However at the same a crisis in the banking system caused a reduction of personal borrowing and limited the availability of consumer credit. For example credit cards were available only to a small percentage of the population. The underdeveloped credit card system, coupled with the financial difficulties in the mid-1990s, accounted for the high percentage of cash payments in business-to-consumer markets. In 2003 more than two thirds of retail exchanges were cash transactions. As bank credit was limited a new market for consumer credit opened up, with retailers offering some customers credit, especially for consumer durables.

Sociodemographic dynamics have played a major part in reshaping retail practices in Mexico. Older consumers are traditional and habitually shop on a daily basis at small local shops called *tiendas abarrotes*. More than 69 per cent of Mexican people are below 30 years of age and those who are employed have less time to shop on a daily basis. Therefore they visit large retail outlets on a weekly basis and *tiendas abarrotes* to supplement their shopping on week days. They have less time for food preparation, which has given rise to greater consumption of ready-to-eat meals and canned, frozen and chilled food. Working women have made a major contribution to this purchasing shift, especially in urban areas. As women are usually in charge of everyday household purchases, most super- and hypermarkets target young working women and women with children.

Rural–urban differences are important to consider. Rural consumers tend to be more conservative in their shopping habits. They still rely on home-grown produce, local stores and open markets. Moreover there is a wide geographical variation in preferences and customs. Every state in Mexico has its own traditions, and consumer behavior differs from state to state. In general, however, Mexicans' shared cultural traditions result in similar purchasing patterns.

Retailing

As in the rest of Latin America, Mexican retail outlets fall into two distinct groups. The first consists of modern outlets with specific target groups, operational efficiencies and advanced technology. The second consists of traditional establishments, many of which are in the informal economy. Mexican retailing is highly fragmented and there is a large number of individual retailers. The consolidation of large retail stores has facilitated access for local producers to the national market. This boosts their sales volumes but reduces their profit margins. The consolidation has also put a lot of pressure on small retailers, many of which are struggling to survive or are being engulfed by larger retailers. However small retailers still serve the needs of the majority of Mexicans.

Traditional food retailers

Traditional food outlets that compete successfully with modern retail chains, super-, hyper- and megamarkets and convenience stores are the public markets (*mercados públicos*) and open-air markets (*tianguis*).

The public markets are permanent, covered and enclosed. They are set up with central and/or local government assistance and the local government usually plays a part in their management. The markets rent space to a large number of independent traders and the total space is divided into designated areas for the different types of merchandise sold.

Public markets are very popular and are widespread in large towns and cities throughout Mexico. In the 1990s there was a continuous increase in the number of such markets. Some are small with fewer than 50 tenants, mostly retailers, while others are very large with more than 5000 wholesale tenants.

The tradition of open-air markets dates back to the pre-Hispanic period, as indicated by their indigenous name, *tianguis*. The *tianguis* are temporary and can be found at crossroads in urban areas. They rarely have central or local government support and move from location to location. The range of goods sold is more diverse than in public markets and includes fresh and preserved food, flowers, clothes, footwear, accessories, toys, books, papers, magazines and spare parts for vehicles. *Tianguis* that sell fresh produce comprise just a few stalls while those offering large assortments of products may comprise several hundred. The number of open-air markets is substantially higher than that of public markets. In Mexico City there are thousands of open-air markets throughout the year.

Tiendas abarrotes are small family-run stores with a limited range of products and are part of the Mexican social culture. The more than 200000 registered *tiendas abarrotes* offer a personal service and enjoy a relationship of trust with their customers. Their supplies come from wholesalers with a country-wide distribution network. The products commonly sold by these stores are milk, bread, confectionary, oil, sugar, potato chips, salt and soap. One of their competitive advantages is that they provide credit to cash-strained customers who cannot obtain credit elsewhere. While consumers from all socioeconomic classes shop in *tiendas abarrotes* they are predominantly used by class C, D and E consumers.

Modern retail outlets and chains

Modern retail outlets have been present in Mexico for decades, but until the 1980s they were few and only served the needs of class A consumers and expatriates. Their goods were up-market and the prices were high. Aggressively expanding supermarkets started to target class B and C consumers, thus extending their customer base to lower-income households. Modern retail outlets mushroomed throughout Mexico in the 1990s and early 2000s. In spite of this growth, aggressive marketing practices are still absent in Mexican retailing.

The price sensitivity of Mexicans has played into the hands of large retailers who have strong bargaining power and can therefore offer a variety of products at discounted prices, sometimes lower than the cost of production. This has contributed to the growth of domestic discount stores and global players such as Wal-Mart, who have engaged in a price competition with established Mexican retailers and small traditional shops.

Supermarkets that sell packaged goods at higher prices than unpackaged ones sold elsewhere, including vegetables, fruit and unpasteurized milk, have not been able to attract mass consumers and have therefore tried to create the image of traditional food markets in their retail outlets. This has had a major effect on the arrangement, display and assortment of food products. The standardization of produce puts supermarkets at a disadvantage because consumers in Mexico are very particular about the ripeness and freshness of fruit and vegetables. Open-air markets have a competitive advantage in this regard as vendors tend to group products according to their freshness, look, color and size, which is not practiced by supermarkets. Because of the high price sensitivity of the average Mexican consumer food retail chains charge approximately the same price for respective commodity food products irrespective of their size, appearance and usefulness as the traders at the public marketplaces and open-air markets.

Consequently competition between retail chains and traditional markets has developed into severe tight price-based rivalry. Retail chains try to match the prices charged by traditional retailers in order to convert traditionalist shoppers into supermarket clients. The price discounts in supermarkets can incur a negative margin but this is offset by the sale of non-discounted items. As traditional retailers already work on low profit margins and do not have the supermarkets' financial strength and economies of scale in storage, distribution and marketing, they cannot match supermarket discounts. Consequently they are losing market share to supermarkets in urban areas, where consumer demand is highly price elastic.

The Mexican companies Grupo Gigante, Controladora Comercial Mexicana and Organización Soriana are major players in the food retail sector and in 2004 they joined forces to fight against the aggressive market penetration by Wal-Mart. This effort was supported by the Mexican government as it was keen to protect domestic retailers and suppliers (Malkin, 2004). Wal-Mart has responded with a low-price strategy.

Wal-Mart started its Mexican operations with a joint venture with Mexico's leading retailer, CIFTRA. In 1997 it bought a controlling stake in CIFTRA and became the largest retailer in Mexico, with stores in more than 70 cities and accounting for about 50 per cent of sales in the sector. In 2000 Wal-Mart gained full control of the management of the company and changed its name to Wal-Mart de Mexico. In 2003 total supermarket sales in Mexico amounted to US$20 billion, US$10.8 billion of which went to Wal-Mart. By that time Wal-Mart owned 687 super stores in 71 cities under the retail brands of Wal-Mart, Aurera-Bodega, Superama and Sam's Club, as well as Suburbias (a more up-market department store chain) and 235 VIP restaurants (Ross, 2005). Wal-Mart mostly targets class A, B and C consumers, unlike in the United States and other developed markets, where it targets low- to middle-income consumers. Mexican supermarket chains are attempting to copy

Wal-Mart's strategy but they do not have the financial or procurement power of the global retailer. The expansion strategies adopted by Wal-Mart have been highly successful, despite the attempt by Mexican retailers to fight jointly against its push for market dominance.

Among the other types of retail stores are megamarkets, which are very large outlets with more than 10000 square meters of floor space. They offer a complete range of groceries and a broad variety of consumer durables such as white goods, as well as a large number of services. Hypermarkets have a shopping area of 5000–10000 square meters and sell a large range of groceries and non-grocery goods, offering a limited number of services.

With a floor space of 2500–5000 meters, *bodegas* sell most grocery and non-grocery product lines to individual customers at wholesale prices. In order to keep prices low they either restrict their offers to products or provide only a very limited range of services. As the goods are piled up on the floor, *bodegas* look like warehouses.

Supermarkets have a shopping area of 500–5000 square meters. They mostly offer perishable goods and grocery products such as food, cosmetics, detergents and toiletries.

So-called membership clubs stock groceries, garments, footwear and so on. Most of the products are sold in bulk or in multiple-unit packs. They sell only to club members and all the prices are wholesale. The premises are large (about 5000 square meters) and the storage and operational costs are relatively low.

A popular retail format to arrive in Mexico is the convenience store. By 2004 there were nearly 5000 such stores with combined annual sales of more than US$2.5 billion. If they continue to expand at the present pace, by the end of 2005 their number will exceed 6000 and sales will reach more than US$3 billion, thus making this retail segment the most dynamic of all (Guthrie, 2005). The convenience stores with the largest presence are 7-Eleven, Oxxo and Extra. The latter is owned by the powerful Mexican brewery group Modelo.

Chain retailers enjoy economies of scale in storage, distribution and marketing, and they can spread their fixed costs over a higher sales volume. These advantages, coupled with lower inventory risk, allow demand efficiencies, provided that supply is strictly managed and controlled. Therefore chain retailers purchase most of their supplies directly from growers or agents, rather than wholesalers. This is slowly eroding the wholesale system, but so far its impact has been limited by consumers' preference for traditional stores and the low income of the majority of the population. Retail chains have also benefited from the strict requirements on packaging, which limit damage to produce and yield savings in the value chain, and the requirements for consistent quality and quality control have brought further cost savings. Traditional wholesalers and small producers find produce sorting difficult, so instead of it being done in rural areas where the cost of labor is low it is conducted in towns, where labor costs are higher. Consequently the wholesalers and producers incur significant losses.

Advertising

Due to the large number of newspapers, radio broadcasters and the extensive television network, Mexico is the media center of Spanish-speaking Latin America. The most influential medium is Televisa, which is part of Telesistema Mexicano, the largest communications conglomerate in the developing world as well as one of the world's major transnational media empires.

The largest newspaper group is Organización Editorial Mexicana (OEM), which owns about 90 newspapers, followed by Novedades Editores, which belongs to Telesistema Mexicano. There are many regional newspapers – Mexico City alone has 15. *Excélsior* is the most prestigious national daily and one of the most trusted newspapers in Latin America.

National broadcasting stations are divided into commercial and cultural networks. All commercial stations are financed by public and private advertising but are obliged to devote 12 per cent of broadcasting time to government-funded promotions and other programs. Political advertising is widespread in all media.

Despite the well developed media infrastructure advertising expenditure is low – less than US$15 per capita in 2002, significantly less than in Argentina, Brazil, Chile and Colombia. The relative share of various media in total advertising expenditure stayed the same in 1997–2002 (Table 5.1) whereas total advertising expenditure almost halved from US$4.3 billion in 1997 to US$2.2 billion in 2002.

Promotional activities in Mexico are multifaceted but are dominated by aspirational advertising that creates positive associations with the lifestyles of rich and powerful celebrities and high achievers in sports. The advertising message usually tries to lure consumers into believing that ownership of the product in question will have a positive effect on the way they perceive themselves. Therefore such advertisements predominantly feature white Europeans and Americans rather than Mexicans. It is believed that people's admiration of American and European lifestyles has forced Mexican companies to refrain from using

Table 5.1 Share of media in advertising expenditure, Mexico, 1997 and 2002 (per cent)

	1997	2002
Television	73	72.0
Radio	11	11.0
Newspapers	8	8.5
Magazines	4	4.0
Outdoor advertising	3	3.0
Cinema	1	0.5

Source: Grupo Radio Centro.

Mexican characters and personalities when they are trying to communicate high product quality. Moreover many of the advertisements shown in Mexico are made in other Latin American countries in order to cut costs. For the same reason they are used throughout the region. Special advertisements are produced for the affluent class A consumers. Class D and E consumers, amounting to about 55 million people, have extremely low purchasing power so are rarely targeted specifically.

Informative advertisements are rare and are usually related to favorable interest rates, insurance policies and so on. Informative advertisements predominantly feature Mexicans who are portrayed as benefiting from cheap car and supermarket credit, store credit cards and payment options. Wal-Mart has used such advertisements in order to broaden its customer base. The advertising regulatory council (Consejo de Autoregulación y Etica Publicitaria, or Conar), deals with complaints about advertisements and ensures that the advertising industry follows the legal regulations and code of ethics. It also serves as a mediator for the resolution of disputes between the makers of advertisements and advertisers, especially in cases where comparative advertising has been used as this has recently become a serious issue in Mexico.

Internet marketing

About 11.5 per cent of Mexican people are connected to the internet, significantly more than the average of 7.6 per cent for the whole of Latin America. Only in Spain and the United States are there more Hispanic internet users. However internet use in Mexico is constrained by people's comparatively low disposable income and the lack of telecommunication infrastructure in rural areas. Moreover limited competition in the telecommunication sector has led to higher call charges, thus further restricting internet penetration. Internet use is mainly confined to the large urban areas, predominantly Mexico City. The limited availability of credit is an important factor in computer purchases, and not all households that do have a computer are connected to the internet. Most internet users are young working adults with a higher than average monthly income and teenagers from class A and B families, plus those educated abroad.

The slow rate of internet adoption has limited the growth of internet marketing. Moreover there is doubt about the security of internet payments and Mexicans continue to prefer face-to-face transactions with trusted retailers. Consumer durables and travel services account for the majority of internet transactions. The auction web site e-Bay is attractive to consumers as it offers extensive choice and bargain prices thus addressing Mexicans' price sensitivity.

Conclusion

Mexico is one of the largest countries in Latin America in terms of territory and population, and one of the largest economies in respect of GDP and the value of foreign trade. While it has attracted sizable FDI flows, the outflow of Mexican FDI has been disproportionately small considering the size and potential of the economy. Powerful US corporations such as Wal-Mart have established themselves in the Mexican market and are posing a threat to domestic companies.

This and the persistent but controllable trade deficit reflect the somewhat passive internationalization of the Mexican economy. As a member of NAFTA, Mexico's sizable foreign trade is largely skewed towards the United States, which accounts for more than 75 per cent of total foreign trade. This has made Mexico vulnerable to fluctuations in the US economy.

Mexico's attractiveness as a destination for FDI is being seriously challenged by the emergence of other large markets, such as China and Brazil, and the withdrawal of manufacturing capital has become a cause of concern for the future development of the national economy.

Another cause of concern is the rapidly increasing size of socioeconomic classes D and E, which together account for more than 50 per cent of the population, almost double the percentage 12 years ago. This has had negative repercussions on the growth of demand. Class D and E consumers are particularly price sensitive, which influences the structure of product and brand offerings and puts pressure on higher value-added consumer goods. However the tendency for brand loyalty among the more affluent class A and B consumers has enabled US brands to gain high levels of market acceptance and brand recognition. While the majority of Mexicans are traditional in their buying behavior, especially in the case of food and well-known domestic products and brands, the producers of such goods have come under pressure from imported or locally produced foreign brands. As a consequence some large Mexican companies have joined forces to withstand the competion by financially strong and more experienced foreign multinationals.

Acknowledgement

Some of the information on marketing in Mexico has kindly been provided by Dr Hyun-Sook Lee Kim of the Istituto Tecnológico y de Estudos Superiores de Monterrey, Mexico.

Recommended reading

Babb, S. (2002) *Managing Mexico: Economists from Nationalism to Neoliberalism* (Princeton, NJ: Princeton University Press).

Crouch, N. (2004) *Mexicans and Americans: Cracking the Cultural Code* (London: Nicholas Brealey) Publishing.

Deaton, G. (ed.) (2003) *The Guide to Mexico for Business*, 11th edn (Mexico City: American Chamber of Commerce of Mexico).

Hakim, P. and R. Litan (eds) (2002) *The Future of North American Integration beyond NAFTA* (New York: Brookings Institution).

Kenna, P. and S. Lacy (1994) *Business Mexico: A Practical Guide to Understanding Mexican Business Culture* (London: Contemporary Books).

Kotabe, M. and R. Leal (eds) (2001) *Market Revolution in Latin America: Beyond Mexico* (Oxford: Pergamon Press).

Piggott, C. (2001) *Mexico: A Market for the 21st Century* (London: Euromoney Institutional Investor PLC).

Reed, G. and R. Gray (1997) *How to Do Business in Mexico: Your Essential and Up-To-Date Guide for Success* (Austin, TX: University of Texas Press).

Williams, M. (ed.) (2001) *Market Reforms in Mexico: Coalitions, Institutions, and the Politics of Policy Changes* (Lanham, MD: Rowman & Littlefield Publishers).

6
Marketing in Peru

Map 5   Peru
Source: www.cia.gov/cia/publications/factbook/geos/pe.html.

Brief historical background

Peru is the birthplace of many civilizations and the Latin American country with the richest historical past. There is evidence that nomadic hunters inhabited the land in 20000 BC. The development of agriculture began in 3000 BC with the cultivation of cotton, chili peppers, beans and squashes, and archaeological findings show that pottery, weaving, fishing and horticulture were well-advanced. The peoples of Moche and Nazca left enigmatic proof of their existence in the form of massive pyramids and the giant Nazca Lines. The indigenous Wari people were militarily strong and conquered and subdued other peoples living in present-day Peru. Subsequently the Chimu, Chachapoyas, Chanka and Cuzco formed independent kingdoms.

In the thirteenth century AD Peru lay at the heart of the vast Inca Empire, one of the greatest empires of its time and the most advanced ancient American civilization.

At the beginning of the sixteenth century the Spaniard Francisco Pizarro landed with his army in northern Ecuador and set about subduing the Incas. While the Incas put up strong resistance the fate of South America was sealed. During the conquest of Peru the Spaniards led by Pizarro founded Lima, which became known as the City of Kings and was at the heart of political, economic, social and cultural events in South America for almost four centuries.

The 1780 rebellion by the Inca nobleman Túpac Amaru II marked the start of a series of uprisings against Spanish rule. In the nineteenth century liberation fighters called Emancipators received assistance from Argentinean soldiers led by General José de San Martín. While Peru's independence from Spain was declared on 28 July 1821, during the next three years Spanish troops fought to regain control. The Spanish colonial armies were eventually defeated by troops headed by Simón Bolívar in the battle of Ayacucho fought on 9 December 1824.

After the liberation of Peru in 1824 there was a long period of political volatility as civilian political leaders and military officers struggled for rule over the country – during the first 32 years of its independence the Republic of Peru had 51 rulers. However in effect it was the economically powerful Peruvians of European descent who dominated the country. These were moneyed landowners who had accumulated their wealth by running large estates worked by Indian serfs. No industrialization took place during this period.

With the help of foreign and domestic capital, mining gradually began to develop. However agriculture continued to be the most important sector, with enslaved Indians laboring in the huge sugar plantations in the coastal area and rubber plantations in the Amazon jungle. After the war with Chile (1879–83) the military ruled Peru for 10 years.

Migration from rural areas to Lima began in the 1920s, when small landowners came under so much pressure from the large landowners that they were forced to leave their now unprofitable farms. Many of them found work in the textile industry, which was booming at that time. The revolutions in Russia and Mexico had a strong ideological and political influence on Peru's emerging working class, which comprised 18 000 people by 1933.

The Great Depression caused a drop in Peru's main agricultural and livestock exports. A consequent plummet in the value of imports was followed by a significant devaluation of the national currency. Peruvian investors diverted capital to other countries because of the volatile domestic economy and market supply became concentrated. Thus by the 1940s, 6 per cent of Peruvian firms controlled 66 per cent of the national market.

In the 1950s and the first half of the 1960s Peru developed a new economic and social identity. Manufacturing was established and haciendas became mechanized, causing mass migration to urban areas, mostly Lima. People expelled from their lands or attracted by education and job opportunities flooded the capital.

In the second half of the 1960s there was considerable social unrest when peasants, inspired by the Cuban Revolution, struggled to recover their land. A military regime led by Velasco Alvarado took power over the country in October 1968. The regime's aim was to develop national capitalism, and agrarian reforms were introduced in an attempt to transform the land-owning feudal class into an efficient industrial bourgeoisie. However the Peruvian landowners were only interested in short-term profits and instead of investing in the country's industrialization deposited their money in foreign banks or invested in non-industrial sectors such as banking, finance and insurance.

In 1978 military rule ended and a new constitution was adopted. The 1980s were unstable politically, economically and socially. During the five-year presidency of Alan Garcia, Peru experienced 2 000 000 per cent inflation and the movement *Sendero Luminoso* (Shining Path) took control of vast swathes of the country after killing the local authorities.

Under President Alberto Fujimori the country enjoyed a dramatic economic turnaround and significant progress was made with curtailing guerrilla activity. Nevertheless the economic slump from the late 1990s generated dissatisfaction with his regime. This, coupled with international pressure and corruption scandals, led to Fujimori's downfall. Since then the economic and political circumstances of the country have improved, with President Toledo introducing greater economic freedom and relinquishing power to the provinces. This has weakened the ability of the central government to create the necessary conditions for sustainable economic development.

Economic overview

The economy of Peru is dual in nature. The official or formal economy is supplemented by non-registered, tax-evading business ventures, drug-related activities and huge remittances from Peruvians working and living abroad. According to the Inter-American Development Bank the latter amounted to about 5 per cent of official GDP in 2003. The official Peruvian economy has always been strongly dominated by powerful business elites of European origin.

In 2000–4 GDP grew at an average rate of 3.5 per cent. However the high rate of population growth slowed down the growth of per capita GDP (Figure 6.1). The formal economy comprises services which account for about two thirds of GDP; industry (mostly mining and manufacturing) contributes about a quarter and the rest is accounted for by agriculture. The fishing industry, which is included in agriculture, has recently grown in significance.

Although the formal Peruvian economy grew in 2004 the impact of this growth was restricted by continuous political and social instability

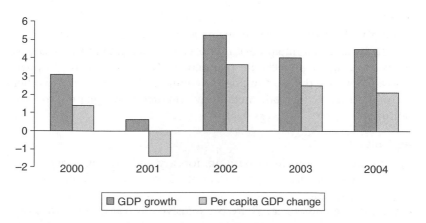

Figure 6.1 Annual growth of GDP and per capita GDP, Peru, 2000–4 (per cent)
Sources: World Bank; International Monetary Fund.

and annual increases in taxation. In 2004 GDP rose by 4.5 per cent, due mainly to the growth of exports and private investment. All productive sectors grew on average by 4.8 per cent, except for agriculture, which fell by more than 1 per cent. Industries with the highest growth rate in 2004 were fishing (18.3 per cent), mining (7.6 per cent) and manufacturing (5.5 per cent). Peruvian exports also grew substantially thanks to rising metal prices.

Employment in the formal economy increased throughout the 1990s with the creation of about 15 million jobs. Official employment rose from 2512600 jobs in 1991 to 8182100 in 2001. The increase was highest in services, followed by agriculture and manufacturing.

The service sector

The formal service sector in Peru includes governmental and private services. Until the mid-1990s the state provided the majority of services and had a virtual monopoly over finance, transportation and telecommunication. Large foreign investments have recently poured into the service sector and the latter has markedly improved. Judged by the value of inputs, government services grew quickly in 1950–2000 and currently account for about 12 per cent of GDP.

Retailing and wholesaling are the most important private service sector activities and accounted for about 22 per cent of GDP in 2002. Financial and business services are next in importance, followed by transportation and communications. Electricity generation and supply and water distribution contribute only a small share of GDP.

Industry

Mining is the most important sector and accounts for 50 per cent of export earnings. Its importance is expected to increase in the future as many investment projects are planned for its development. Copper, gold and zinc are the most important commodities exported. The other main industries are food, metallurgy, textiles and apparel, and oil refining.

Agriculture

Agriculture in Peru includes farming, forestry and fishing. Crops raised along the coastal area account for about 15 per cent of export revenue. The principal agricultural products are sugar cane, potatoes, rice, maize, cotton, coffee and wheat. There is extensive cultivation of coca, from which the drug cocaine is extracted. Livestock farmers raise llamas, vicunas, cattle, sheep, goats, pigs, horses, mules and poultry.

Farming in Peru is fragmented, with many small farms that are predominantly self-sufficient. Large farms, many of which are cooperatives, produce food for national distribution or export.

The informal economy

Peru has a huge informal economy that provides employment for more than 50 per cent of the total urban labor force. According to de Soto *et al.* (1986), 38 per cent of GDP and 60 per cent of total working hours were associated with the informal economy in the 1980s, and the OIT (2002) estimates that the informal economy employed nearly 60 per cent of the workforce in 2001. This explains the enormous macroeconomic problem currently faced by the Peruvian government. The informal economy is an important means of survival for a large proportion of the population. It also accounts for a high proportion of personal and retail services, and for a considerable volume of industrial production.

The expansion of the informal economy began in the 1960s when the government imposed intolerable taxation rates and costs on registered businesses (de Soto, 1989). Another reason for its rapid growth has been the slow development of the formal economy compared with the growth and urbanization of the population. The informal economy ranges from street vending, mostly in urban areas, to assembling computers from discarded spare parts.

Successive governments have attempted to find ways to curb the informal economy. They have tried to crack down on unregistered vendors and their sources of supply, and to encourage the formalization of businesses by providing information and technical and financial help. However it is now officially recognized that the informal economy is an inseparable and integral part of the overall economy and provides a living for a great number of people who lack viable alternatives, even though it does not contribute towards health care, education and other basic public services. As legally registered businesses have to pay taxes and informal economic activities are tax free, competition among formal and informal businesses is based on different foundations, which creates tension among the players. Formal businesses can be divided into two distinct groups. Those in the first group reduce their costs by subcontracting activities to businesses in the informal economy, thus illegally benefiting from tax free inputs that increase their profits. Those in the second group distance themselves from the informal economy and view the latter as an impediment to the economic growth and stability of Peru.

Construction (especially of residential areas), commerce, the production of textiles, clothing, furniture and so on, and automotive repair are the most common informal operations in Peru (Ghersi, 1997).

A study of the pricing and advertising strategies of small entrepreneurs (Zuin, 2004) has found that such entrepreneurs engage in price reductions but this is restricted by profit-making considerations. Thus informal companies' efforts to increase their market share is more likely to be based on word-of-mouth advertising than profit margin minimization. It is interesting to note that almost 87 per cent of the entrepreneurs interviewed stated that they had used their own savings to start their operations, and the majority invested all or part of their profits in expanding their business. Any profits that were saved were rarely deposited in banks.

Drug-related activities

A large number of Peruvian people cultivate coca. Until 1996 Peru was the largest coca growing area in the world and the value of the coca produced was estimated to be two thirds of that of legal agricultural produce (McClintock, 1990). The present government has developed alternative means of livelihood in the leading coca-growing areas in an effort to convince the farmers not to grow the crop. The success of this means that the significance of drug-related activities in Peru has diminished.

Foreign trade

According to the Economist Intelligence Unit (2005), in 2004 exports reached US$12.5 billion and imports US$9.8 billion, thus establishing a positive trade balance (Table 6.1).

Peru has a comparative advantage in fishing and metal extraction, and exports of fishmeal and metal account for about two thirds of total exports. The fishing industry is huge but highly cyclical and in need of modernization. The value of the principal goods exported from and imported to Peru in 2004 is shown in Table 6.2.

Table 6.1 Foreign trade, Peru, 2000–4 (US$ billion)

	2000	2001	2002	2003	2004
Exports	6.9	7.0	7.4	8.9	12.5
Imports	7.3	7.2	7.7	8.3	9.8
Trade balance	−0.4	−0.2	−0.3	0.6	2.7

Sources: World Bank; International Monetary Fund.

Table 6.2 Value of principal exports and imports, Peru, 2004 (US$ billion)

Exports	Value	Imports	Value
Copper	2.446	Intermediate goods	5.358
Gold	2.362	Capital goods	2.366
Fishmeal	1.103	Consumer goods	1.980

Source: Economist Intelligence Unit (2005).

Peru's main export markets are the United States, Switzerland and China. In 2003 the United States received 27.1 per cent of the total volume of exports and in 2004 it received 25.9 per cent, followed by Switzerland and China with 7.7 per cent each in 2003 and 7.9 per cent in 2004. In the case of imports, the United States accounted for 28.6 per cent in 2003 and 24.1 per cent in 2004. Recently Peru has received a significant volume of imports from Spain and a number of Latin American countries, including Chile, Brazil and Colombia. The structure of imports in 2001 is shown in Table 6.3.

The import regime in Peru has been liberalized and in theory imports are rarely subject to restrictions, apart from the labeling and packaging regulations imposed on some goods. Nevertheless in 2003 Peru's foreign trade policy and regime were characterized by arbitrary government intervention, unsound and/or poorly enforced property rights, inefficient

Table 6.3 Structure of imports, Peru, 2001 (per cent)

	Percentage of total
Electrical and electronic goods, machinery, equipment, etc.	27.65
Chemicals and pharmaceuticals	18.01
Crude oil, petroleum, lubricants	13.52
Transportation vehicles	6.55
Metals and metal products (mainly iron and steel)	6.24
Grain, fruit and vegetables, meat, fish, other unprocessed food	6.19
Processed food, milk, fats and oils, sugar, soft drinks, alcohol, cocoa	5.06
Textiles and apparel	4.29
Paper and paper products, cardboard, wood paste, printed material	4.18
Rubber and rubber products	2.01
Other	6.31

Sources: Ministry of Economy of Peru; Peruvian Association of Exporters and Importers.

bureaucracy and red tape. The government has banned the importation of used clothing and shoes unless they are to be distributed free to the poorest members of society. To protect local industries and personal safety the importation of a number of used consumer durables, such as cars that are more than five years old, is also banned. Moreover the importation of agricultural chemicals has recently come under government control and regulation.

The basic *ad valorem* duty is around 12 per cent for most goods, but can vary from 4 per cent to 20 per cent for different product categories. A value-added tax of 18 per cent is levied on all domestic sales transactions. In addition products that fall into the category of luxury goods are subject to a special selective consumption tax, which varies according to the type of product in question. While Peru's import tariffs are somewhat higher than those of its neighboring countries, as a member of the Andean Community it has had to harmonize its tariffs with those imposed by the other member states and it has reduced its import taxes over the years. A common external tariff for the Andean Community was introduced in 2003.

Foreign direct investment

A major priority of the government is to attract more FDI and stimulate domestic investment in all sectors of the formal economy. After a tiny FDI inflow in the 1980s there was a massive influx of capital in the 1990s, amounting to almost US$16 billion. FDI in that period came mostly from Spain and the United States. Mining and energy generation attracted 35 per cent of total FDI, with US FDI going primarily into the mining sector. Its stock by the end of 2002 was US$3.2 billion.

FDI has fluctuated since 1996 but the general trend has been downward. In the meantime FDI outflow has been negligible or non-existent (Figure 6.2). What little there was went to Latin American countries. Despite the small size of outward FDI, Peru ranked eighth among the Latin American states that invested abroad in 1999–2003.

With the implementation of programs for economic stabilization and liberalization the government has removed all restrictions on capital inflow. It has also signed investment promotion and protection agreements with many member countries of the European Union, namely Germany, the Netherlands, Denmark, the United Kingdom, Sweden, Finland, France and Italy.

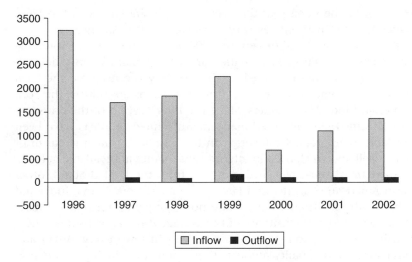

Figure 6.2 FDI inflows and outflows, Peru, 1996–2002 (US$ million)
Sources: UNCTAD; EIU.

Market characteristics and consumer behavior

With a population of 27.5 million in 2003 and a territory of 1285220 square kilometers, Peru is the fifth largest Latin American state. According to Williamson (2003) the literacy rate in Peru is higher than the average for Latin America, but life expectancy is lower and infant mortality is higher. The country ranked seventh in the region in 2003 in terms of GDP, which amounted to US$60.6 billion (Figure 6.3).

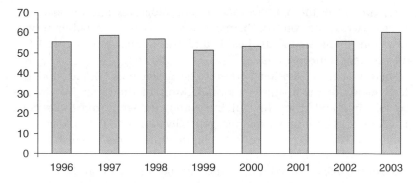

Figure 6.3 GDP, Peru, 1996–2003 (US$ billion)
Sources: UNCTAD; EIU.

However in the same year the average per capita GDP was US$2205, which was 20.5 per cent below the average for Latin America. The market potential of Peru in 2004 was greater than in Colombia and Venezuela. Business activities are predominantly customer oriented. Domestically produced products satisfy the needs of the local market and some go for export. Imported goods are sold in the consumer and industrial markets. Since the liberalization of the economy in the early 1990s, internationally manufactured products have been available in all product categories. In the case of consumer goods most of the well-known global and international brands are available in Peru.

Apart from well-established products from the United States, other Latin American countries and Europe, products from China, India and other Southeast Asian countries are now competing for market share. Because of the price sensitivity of the average Peruvian consumer, inexpensive Chinese goods have found success in low-income urban and rural areas. Better quality products that command a high price are purchased by class A and B consumers. These include a limited range of domestic products and a broad range of imported generic and branded goods. While international luxury brands such as Rolex and Gucci are present in the country they can only be afforded by class A consumers. Premium imported brands are targeted at class A and B consumers, but purchases are more occasional than regular.

There are three distinct areas in Peru, each with its own culture. The Andean area covers a quarter of the country's territory and is inhabited by about 50 per cent of the population. Because of its rugged terrain it has been difficult to develop the region and form its inhabitants into a coherent society. The remainder of the population lives in arid deserts and a small proportion (about 6 per cent) in the Amazon jungle. The latter consists of many tribes that are ethnologically and linguistically diverse. Across the country there are large disparities in public service provision, living standards, health and educational services, and law enforcement is inconsistent.

There is a huge division between the indigenous peoples and the descendants of the Spanish colonials. Most of the latter live in the capital Lima and enjoy high living standards, while the indigenous peoples live in poor rural areas and generally adhere to their old cultural traditions. They engage in primitive agriculture or craftsmanship on a family basis, mostly in extended families called *ayllu*. There are also *mestizos* (people of mixed Indian and European descent) and a comparatively small number of Chinese, Japanese and black people of African descent. The current population structure is 45 per cent Indian, 37 per cent *mestizo*, 15 per cent white (mostly of Spanish descent) and 3 per cent others.

The Andean population consists of two ethno-linguistic groups, one of which speaks Quechua and the other Aymara. Most of the people living in the Andes are extremely poor. Because many in the younger generations crave access to education, electricity, running water and proper sewage systems, which are scarce in most parts of the Andes, there is urban migration on a massive scale.

A middle class started to form in Lima and other large urban areas in the 1970s with the development and modernization of parts of the country and diversification of the economy. Disparity in income distribution has been increasing since the mid-1980s. According to the World Bank the richest 20 per cent of the population have more than 50 per cent of the purchasing power while the poorest 20 per cent have just 4 per cent. Although poverty is decreasing, about six million people can barely afford basic necessities.

Low-income consumers from classes C, D and E with a monthly household income of less than US$250 comprise more than 80 per cent of the population. They are extremely price sensitive and mostly brand indifferent. However they are highly demanding about product quality, especially in the case of food products. High-income consumers (classes A and B) have an average household monthly income of US$900 or more and make up about 5 per cent of the population. One third of the population and the majority of affluent people live in Lima. The latter accounts for nearly 66 per cent of the national income and 80 per cent of the value of food sales in Peru.

Peruvians value domestically produced food because they perceive it to be of better quality and taste than imported food, which is viewed as offering greater variety but is often more expensive. Class A and B consumers buy their food predominantly from supermarkets while class C, D and E consumers prefer to buy it from traditional open markets and grocery stores. While high- and middle-income consumers tend to shop once a week, low-income consumers shop once or twice a day.

Food retail

The food retail market in Peru consists of traditional and modern outlets with sales of US$4.4 billion in 2004. Super- and hypermarket chains account for about 25 per cent of food sales in Lima and almost 20 per cent of total food sales. Traditional open markets and grocery stores account for the remainder.

The share of imported food is small: in the range of 5–7 per cent of total sales. Chile, Colombia, Argentina, Mexico and Brazil account for about 66 per cent of the value of all food imports, and the United States for 8–10 per cent. Most of the food is imported directly by retailers.

The Wong Group and Supermercados Peruanos own the major supermarket and hypermarket chains (Table 6.4). The Wong Group almost exclusively sells food that has been grown or manufactured in Peru whereas about 10 per cent of the food sold by Supermercados Peruanos is imported. The two companies have engaged in severe price wars to gain market share.

The clear market leader, the Wong Group, targets all socioeconomic groups. Its supermarket chain Wong targets high-income class A and B consumers by offering a customer oriented service and a combination of local and foreign products, while its Metro chain of super- and hypermarkets target middle-income class C consumers and low-income class D and E consumers. Here the quality of customer service is lower and all goods are domestically produced. The Wong Group has recently introduced an internet service to enable Peruvians living abroad to buy products for their relatives in Peru.

The chain Supermercados Santa Isabel was owned by the Ahold Group until December 2003, when it was bought by the powerful Peruvian financial company Interbank Group. In March 2004 the name of the holding company was changed to Supermercados Peruanos. In order to build up a larger customer base the latter intends to progressively change its Santa Isabel outlets, which target mostly class A consumers, to Plaza Vea hypermarkets which focus on class B and C consumers. With this strategic move the company expects to grow its operations opening a number of new hypermarket outlets and drawing upon a larger consumer base. Supermercados Peruanos also own the discount chain Minisol, which offers a limited range of basic food products to class D and E consumers.

Table 6.4   Characteristics of super- and hypermarket chains, Lima, 2004

Company	Retail chain name	Ownership	Sales (US$ million)	Market share (%)	Number of outlets
Wong Group	Wong Metro	Peruvian	640	64	27
Supermercados Peruanos	Santa Isabel, Plaza Vea, Minisol	Peruvian	320	32	35
Saga Falabella	Tottus	Chilean	40	4	3

Source: Adapted from Class & Asociados database.

The Chilean retail company Saga Falabella owns the hypermarket chain Tottus, which focuses on class C, D and E consumers and offers local and imported food. As these socioeconomic groups constitute the largest consumer base in Peru the company is planning to expand to most towns in the country.

Convenience stores have recently gained popularity. They are normally located at gas stations and most of their sales revenue comes from alcoholic drinks, tobacco, soft drinks and snacks. The principal convenience store chains are Selects and Mobil Marts (both of which have joint US–Peruvian ownership) and the Peruvian-owned Centauro Grifos.

Traditional food outlets command 80 per cent of food sales in Peru. They consist of about 230 000 grocery stores and approximately 3000 open markets. Almost 45 per cent of the grocery stores and more than 50 per cent of the open markets are in Lima. Open market operators compete with the supermarkets by offering more choice and better customer service.

Advertising and market research

The three largest Peruvian advertising agencies are BBDO Perú, Causa and Merino. Their clients include large multinationals such as Nestlé, Nissan and KFC, local companies such as Cindel and Perúfarma, and other firms with international operations. Advertising agencies in Peru offer a variety of services that encompass all forms of promotion. Specialization is rather limited.

Market research is mostly carried out by the domestic companies CCR Information Resources, Compañiá Peruana de Investigación de Mercados y Opinión Pública, Grupo Apoyo, Ibope Time Perú and Michelsen Consulting. All of these conduct research on marketing and marketing practices and some offer other specialized services. For example CCR Information Resources publishes a monthly on-line bulletin on the market trends for various product categories and brands, Compañiá Peruana de Investigación de Mercados y Opinión Pública conducts periodic studies of consumer preferences in the major urban areas, and Grupo Apoyo conducts research on market trends and customer preferences in the business-to-business and business-to-consumer markets.

Ibope Time Perú is the market leader in media research and offers a diverse range of marketing research services. Michelsen Consulting's many services include on-line advertising and identification of opportunities for business development in the country. The latter is invaluable to new market entrants and companies wishing to expand.

The print media include newspapers and magazines that cater to a variety of readers. There are 45 daily newspapers, seven of which are available on-line. Thirty-one of them are published in Lima and the rest are regional. There are also specialist publications such as the daily *Gestión*, which covers business and economic matters. Three of the newspapers – *Lima Post*, *Peru Times* and *Latin American Press* – are published in English to cater to expatriates. The demographic diversity of the Peruvian population is reflected in the existence of *Prensa Nikkei*, a newspaper for Japanese Peruvians.

The range of magazines is diverse; some of are generalist and some specialized. *Peru Finance* is an English language magazine that covers financial issues, *Punto del Equilibrio* is published in Spanish and addresses business and economic matters, and *17.65%* is an advertising magazine targeted at the general public.

The largest radio station is Radio Nacional del Perú, which broadcasts nationwide. It competes against 31 round-the-clock broadcasters and nearly 100 commercial radio stations. The latter are mostly located in Lima.

Television broadcasters comprise one national TV station that offers limited advertising time and six private channels that account for the bulk of TV advertising. América and RedTV have the highest number of commercials per minute.

Internet advertisements have a low penetration rate due to limited computer access across the country. Few rural households have computers and only a small number of urban households are connected to the internet. It is estimated that only 55 000 individuals engaged in internet shopping in 2003, or just 2.1 per cent of the population.

Advertising expenditure almost doubled in 1997–2004, rising from US$1.08 billion to US$2.12 billion. Expenditure by medium in Latin America and Peru is shown in Table 6.5.

Table 6.5 Advertising expenditure in Latin America and Peru, by medium, 2003 (per cent)

	Latin America	Peru
TV	60	85
Newspapers	19	5
Radio	11	5
Magazines	6	1
Outdoor	3	1
Cinema	1	3

Source: Latin American Media & Marketing (www.zonalatina.com).

Conclusion

Peru dominated the political and economic life of South America for more than three centuries and was home to much of the continent's wealth. Today it is a land of contrasts, with a small percentage of rich people and millions of very poor, a struggling formal economy but flourishing informal economy, and a unique historical heritage but underdeveloped infrastructure.

Recent governments have attempted to curb informal economic activities by increasing the number of jobs in public and private registered businesses. Although this effort has had some success, according to official estimates at the end of 2004 about 55 per cent of the active population was employed in the informal economy. At the same time urban unemployment was running at 10 per cent and rural unemployment at more than 30 per cent. The formal economy has recently experienced tempered growth, with moderate GDP growth by developing economy standards but an insignificant increase in GDP per capita.

Foreign trade has generally been on the rise. Exports consist mainly of primary products and food while imports are strongly dominated by industrial products. There is a dire need for improvements in the trade regime, trade legislation and trade-related practices to facilitate trade growth.

While some industries – such as communications, mining and energy – and a number of services have received large amounts of FDI, sectors such as supermarket retailing are almost exclusively under Peruvian ownership. Outward FDI is small and goes mainly to neighboring Latin American countries. Thus the Peruvian economy has experienced limited, mostly passive, internationalization restricting the international competitiveness of the country.

The consumer market is strongly dominated by traditional retail outlets that mainly sell fast moving consumer goods and locally produced food. The majority of consumers are extremely price sensitive and brand indifferent. Moreover the average purchasing power is low so luxury goods and premium brands have a very small customer base.

Peru has enormous potential to develop new investment opportunities in mining, agriculture, forestry, agricultural machinery, textiles, apparel, fishing and tourism. If an economic strategy to promote these sectors were combined with further liberalization and developmental planning, the economic performance of the country would improve considerably and this would have positive implications for business-to-business and business-to-consumer marketing activities.

Recommended reading

Arce, M. (2005) *Market Reform in Society: Post-Crisis Politics and Economic Change in Authoritarian Peru* (University Park, PA: Penn State University Press).

De Diaz-Limaco, J. (1998) *Peru in Focus: A Guide to the People, Politics and Culture* (New York, NY: Interlink Books).

Peru Country Study Guide (2002) (Washington, DC: International Business Publications).

Peru Export–Import Trade and Business Directory (2004) (Lightning Source UK).

Sheahan, J. (1999) *Searching for a Better Society: Peruvian Economy since 1950* (University Park, PA: Penn State University Press).

Wise, C. (2003) *Reinventing the State: Economic Strategy and Institutional Change in Peru* (Whitewater, Mich.: University of Michigan Press).

Ypeij, A. (1999) *Producing against Poverty: Female and Male Micro-entrepreneurs in Lima, Peru* (Amsterdam: Amsterdam University Press).

7
Concluding Remarks

The countries of Latin America share common historical, cultural and linguistic characteristics and some similarities in economic and social development. When the colonial powers left the region the newly independent countries had relatively similar political and economic structures. Agriculture was the backbone of all the economies and industry made only a small contribution to national wealth as it was slow to develop. The role of the state in the economy and society was substantial, defined not only by the specifics of each country but also by the type of government in question. Most of the countries came under military dictatorship at some point in time, often in response to economic instability or to prevent leftist parties or movements from gaining power. The differences between the countries in size, human power and natural factor endowments created divergent forces and resulted in today's economic and market heterogeneity in the region.

The region is one of the biggest emerging markets in the world in terms of investment and market potential. However until recently the economic strategies of most of the countries were based on import substitution. Their inward-looking economic programs prevented technological advancement and transfer, thus limiting the international competitiveness of their economies, industries and companies. Import substitution was followed by neoliberalist policies based on market liberalization and privatization to encourage competition, increase foreign investment flows and intensify foreign trade. Chile, Mexico, Brazil and Argentina benefited most from these open market-oriented economic policies. Meanwhile the setting up of regional economic integration blocs facilitated the movement of goods, technology and capital.

Despite these positive developments, knowledge-intensive and high-technology businesses are rare and the internationalization of Latin

American economies is mostly confined to exporting primary products or serving as a low-cost production base. Nevertheless Brazil, Chile and Argentina have adopted a proactive approach to the internationalization of key national enterprises, significantly increasing the participation of these economies in foreign operations through FDI in developed and other developing markets. Mexican companies have also increased their international involvement, predominantly via exports to the United States.

The industrial market in Latin America is limited and mostly depends on imports from developed economies such as the United States and member countries of the European Union. Industrial imports from developed countries constitute the largest proportion of imports in all Latin American states, thus ensuring technology transfer and upgrading. They also facilitate assembly operations and the participation of local companies in international supply networks.

The neoliberal economic policies have not yet resulted in significant social improvements. The middle- and low-income social classes have fluctuated in size and income level, and as the role of the state has diminished, families need two wage earners to cover the rising cost of social security, education, health care and everyday necessities. While economic performance has generally improved, Latin Americans still have to live in complex social structures characterized with enormous income disparities. The purchasing power of the average consumer has been severely eroded and the large gap between the haves and have-nots has widened, with the former accumulating more wealth and the latter finding it ever more difficult to make ends meet.

When coupled with economic uncertainty and population diversity, this has had major implications for the marketing strategies of companies that target the mass market. There has been constant pressure for cost reduction by various means, as well as profit margin minimization and brand development. Due to their comparatively high price many established global and international brands have failed in a number of Latin American markets. These brands have been put under immense pressure by domestic products and private label brands, referred to as B brands which offer reasonably high quality at a low price. They have developed a good reputation among consumers and have therefore increased their market share. The other end of the market is served mostly by upscale products and brands that meet the demand of A and B class consumers who have remained loyal to sophisticated brands of foreign and domestic origin. It is in the upscale market where the concept of value for money, as interpreted in developed economies, finds acceptance and support.

The peoples of the region have adjusted to political and economic volatility in different ways. Continuous migration from rural to urban areas and from poorer to richer countries has brought about changes in lifestyle, occupation, education and family life. Latin Americans' traditional family values have been reinforced by economic hardship. This has preserved the importance of household income as a key indicator of purchasing power. Presently families are composed of several generations, where employed and unemployed, conservative and cosmopolitan live together, share their income with the rest of the family and purchasing priorities are decided jointly. Economic cycles and volatility has not only strained household income but also changed the structure of the market. The fragmentation, volatility and market dynamics in Latin America require regional and country-tailored marketing strategies that reflect the complexity and particularities of the region.

Appendix Area, population, main natural resources and GDP of Latin American countries

Table A.1 Caribbean basin

Country	Area (sq. km)	Population in 2003	Main natural resources	GDP composition by sector (%)	GDP per capita (PPP in US$)
Antigua and Barbuda	443	68 300	Climate attracts tourists	Agriculture (4), industry (12), services (84) (2001)	9 690 (2000)
Aruba	193	71 200	Sandy beaches	Agriculture (n.a.), industry (n.a.), services (n.a.)	28 000 (2002)
Bahamas	13 940	299 700	Salt, aragonite, timber, arable land	Agriculture (3), industry (7), services (90) (2001)	16 700 (2003)
Barbados	431	278 300	petroleum, fish, natural gas	Agriculture (6), industry (16), services (78) (2000)	16 200 (2003)
Cayman Islands	262	43 100	Fish, climate, beaches	Agriculture (1), industry (3), services (96) (1999)	35 000 (2002)

Cuba	110 860	11 308 800	Cobalt, nickel, iron, chromium, copper, oil, arable land	Agriculture (6), industry (27), services (67) (2003)	2 900 (2003)
Dominica	754	69 300	Timber, hydroelectric power, arable land	Agriculture (18), industry (24), services (58) (2002)	5 400 (2002)
Dominican Republic	48 730	8 833 700	Nickel, bauxite, gold, silver	Agriculture (11), industry (32), services (57) (2003)	6 000 (2003)
Grenada	344	89 400	Timber, tropical fruit, deepwater harbors	Agriculture (8), industry (24), services (68) (2000)	5 000 (2002)
Guadeloupe	1 780	444 500	Beaches and climate	Agriculture (15), industry (17), services (68) (1997)	8 000 (2003)
Haiti	27 750	7 656 200	Bauxite, copper, calcium carbonate, gold, marble, hydroelectric power	Agriculture (30), industry (20), services (50) (2001)	1 600 (2003)
Jamaica	10 991	2 713 100	Bauxite, gypsum, limestone	Agriculture (7), industry (37), services (56) (2003)	3 900 (2003)
Martinique	1 100	429 500	Coastal scenery and beaches, arable land	Agriculture (6), industry (11), services (83) (1997)	14 400 (2001)
Puerto Rico	9 104	3 898 000	Copper, nickel; potential for oil	Agriculture (1), industry (46), services (53) (2002)	16 800 (2003)

Table A.1 (Continued)

Country	Area (sq. km)	Population in 2003	Main natural resources	GDP composition by sector (%)	GDP per capita (PPP in US$)
Saint Kitts and Nevis	261	38 836	Arable land	Agriculture (4), industry (26), services (70) (2001)	8 800 (2002)
Saint Lucia	616	164 200	Forests, sandy beaches, pumice, mineral springs	Agriculture (7), industry (20), services (73) (2002)	5 400 (2002)
Saint Vincent and the Grenadines	389	117 200	Hydroelectric power, arable land	Agriculture (10), industry (26), services (64) (2001)	2 900 (2002)
Trinidad and Tobago	5 128	1 096 600	Petroleum, natural gas, asphalt	Agriculture (3), industry (49), services (48) (2003)	9 500 (2003)
Turks and Caicos Islands	430	19 960	Spiny lobster, conch	Agriculture (n.a.), industry (n.a.), services (n.a.)	9 600 (2000)
Virgin Islands	352	108 800	Sandy beaches	Agriculture (1), industry (19), services (80) (2003)	17 200 (2002)

Table A.2   Central America

Country	Area (sq. km)	Population in 2003	Main natural resources	GDP composition by sector (%)	GDP per capita (PPP in US$)
Belize	22 966	272 950	Timber, fish, hydroelectric power	Agriculture (23), industry (25), services (52) (2003)	4 900 (2002)
Costa Rica	51 100	3 956 500	Hydroelectric power	Agriculture (9), industry (29), services (62) (2003)	9 100 (2003)
El Salvador	21 040	6 587 500	Hydroelectric power, geothermal power, petroleum, arable land	Agriculture (9), industry (32), services (59) (2003)	4 800 (2003)
Guatemala	108 890	14 280 600	Petroleum, nickel, rare wood, fish, hydroelectric power	Agriculture (23), industry (19), services (58) (2003)	4 100 (2003)
Honduras	112 090	6 823 600	Timber, gold, silver, copper, lead, zinc, iron ore, antimony, coal, fish, hydroelectric power	Agriculture (13), industry (32), services (55) (2003)	2 600 (2003)
Nicaragua	129 494	5 359 800	Gold, silver, copper, tungsten, lead, zinc, timber, fish	Agriculture (29), industry (25), services (46) (2003)	2 300 (2003)
Panama	78 200	3 000 500	Copper, mahogany, timber, shrimp, hydroelectric power	Agriculture (8), industry (15), services (77) (2003)	6 300 (2003)

Table A.3 North America

Country	Area (sq. km)	Population in 2003	Main natural resources	GDP composition by sector (%)	GDP per capita (PPP in US$)
Mexico	1 972 550	105 000 000	Petroleum, silver, copper, gold, lead, zinc, natural gas, timber	Agriculture (4), industry (26), services (70) (2003)	9 000 (2003)

Table A.4 South America

Country	Area (sq. km)	Population in 2003	Main natural resources	GDP composition by sector (%)	GDP per capita (PPP in US$)
Argentina	2 766 890	39 144 800	Fertile plains, lead, zinc, tin, copper, iron ore, manganese, petroleum, uranium	Agriculture (11), industry (35), services (54) (2003)	11 200 (2003)
Bolivia	1 098 580	8 724 156	Tin, natural gas, petroleum, zinc, tungsten, antimony, silver, iron, lead, gold, timber, hydroelectric power	Agriculture (15), industry (33), services (52) (2003)	2 400 (2003)
Brazil	8 511 965	184 101 100	Bauxite, gold, iron ore, manganese, nickel, phosphates, platinum, tin, uranium, petroleum, hydroelectric power, timber	Agriculture (10), industry (39), services (51) (2003)	7 600 (2003)
Chile	756 950	15 825 000	Copper, timber, iron ore, nitrates, precious metals, molybdenum, hydroelectric power	Agriculture (7), industry (39), services (54) (2003)	9 900 (2003)

Country			Natural resources	GDP composition	GDP per capita
Colombia	1 138 910	42 310 800	Petroleum, natural gas, coal, iron ore, nickel, gold, copper, emeralds, hydroelectric power	Agriculture (14), industry (32), services (54) (2003)	6 300 (2003)
Ecuador	283 560	13 212 700	Petroleum, fish, timber, hydroelectric power	Agriculture (9), industry (30), services (61) (2003)	3 300 (2003)
French Guiana	91 000	191 300	Bauxite, timber, gold, petroleum, fish, niobium, tantalum	Agriculture (n.a.), industry (n.a.), services (n.a.)	8 300 (2001)
Guyana	214 970	705 800	Bauxite, gold, diamonds, timber, shrimp, fish	Agriculture (37), industry (23), services (40) (2003)	4 000 (2003)
Paraguay	406 750	6 191 500	Hydroelectric power, timber, iron ore, manganese, limestone	Agriculture (25), industry (24), services (51) (2003)	4 700 (2003)
Peru	1 285 220	27 545 000	Copper, silver, gold, petroleum, timber, fish, iron ore, coal, phosphate, potash, hydroelectric power, natural gas	Agriculture (8), industry (27), services (65) (2003)	5 100 (2003)
Suriname	163 270	437 000	Timber, hydroelectric power, fish, bauxite, gold, copper, platinum, iron ore	Agriculture (13), industry (22), services (65) (2001)	4 000 (2003)
Uruguay	176 220	3 399 300	Arable land, hydroelectric power	Agriculture (7), industry (27), services (66) (2003)	12 800 (2003)
Venezuela	912 050	25 017 400	Petroleum, natural gas, iron ore, gold, bauxite, other minerals, hydroelectric power, diamonds	Agriculture (5), industry (50), services (45) (2004)	4 800 (2003)

Notes

1. This chapter is based on *Robles et al.* (2003).
2. Some observers of market trends suggest that the middle class of Latin America lives in the United States.
3. A common estimate of variability is the standard deviation of the series.
4. See www.census.gov/populations/so...hispanic/cps98/98gifsshow/sld009.htm.
5. See www.zonalatina.com/Zldata161.htm.
6. This statement is based on Gini coefficients. The Gini index measures the extent to which the distribution of income among households or individuals within an economy deviates from a perfectly equal distribution. A Gini index of zero represents perfect equality. The higher the number the larger the inequality. An index of 1.0 represents perfect inequality or one person owning all income.
7. See also www.strategyresearch.com/IS_Latin_america_marketing.htm.
8. For instance in Argentina in 2001 it had a market share of about 35 per cent in all categories. For food the share was 50 per cent. See 'Revolucion en el universo de marcas', *Mercado*, 2 January 2001.
9. Brazil is the only country in the region where inflation increased in 1999. This was due to the depreciation of the real in 1998.
10. For more details of specific changes see *Qué Pasa*, June 1999; Ten key consumption trends in Argentina – 2000; Argentine youth in 21st century; (www.adlatina.com); Materialism in Latin America, *TGI Latina*; and Buying clothes in Brazil, *TGI Brazil*; (www.zonalatina.com).
11. Socioeconomic classifications vary across Latin America. In order to establish a pan-regional classification to allow intraregional comparisons, the consumer research organization Media and Markets in Latin America has identified four groups of consumers: A, B, C and D. The variables used for the classification include household income, educational level and possession of certain household goods. Socioeconomic class A comprises households with the most spending power, college education and high ownership of household goods. The other classes are upper-middle (B), middle (C) and working class and poor (D). Families living in extreme poverty are not included in the classification. Each class is divided into two or three subgroups. According to the Strategy Research Corporation, in Latin America on average 2 per cent of people are in the upper class, 12 per cent in the upper-middle class, 30 per cent in the middle class and 56 per cent in the working class. www.zonalatina.com/Z1data07.htm; Strategy Research Corporation (2001).
12. General Motors is targeting middle-class consumers with its European made car the Astra. The Astra is available in Brazil, Mexico, Argentina, Chile and Venezuela.
13. Banco Itau, Annual Report, 1999.
14. See 'El Mercado de las telecomunicaciones en la Argentina', www.adlatina.com/pages/invest.php.
15. The average number of hours of TV watching varies little across Latin America.

16. See 'Bombril, Icono de la cultura brasileña', www.adlatina.com/pages/investigaciones/invest.php.
17. See 'Telenovelas and Soap in Latin America', www.zonalatina.com/z1data 131.htm.
18. See R. Soong and D. Verdin, 'Is there a Latin American audience for regional media?', www.zonalatina.com/Z1data05.htm; *'Kotzrinker*, Viaja bien el contenido?', www.baquia.com/com/legacy/13301.html.
19. This section is based on Hatten and Korsun (2000).
20. See www.hispanicbusiness.com/news/news_print.asp?id = 2898.
21. See www.idgnow.uol.com.br/idgnow/internet/2001/03/0060.
22. R. Soong, 'Latin American Internet Activities', www.zonalatina.com, 18 December 1999.
23. See www.ebusinessforum.com.
24. Self-service stores include supermarkets, hypermarkets, department stores and convenience stores.
25. For a detailed account of Carrefour's international expansion see Sternquist (1997).
26. Exxel has since fallen into financial difficulty and is in the process of divesting several businesses. See *Clarin*, 24 September 2001.
27. The Dutch hypermarket group Makro entered Colombia before Carrefour but had little success.
28. Farmacias Ahumada established its Brazilian network by acquiring a controlling interest in the pharmaceutical chain Drogamed. See *Business Latin America*, 1 May 2000.

Bibliography

Aaker, D. and E. Joachimsthaler (2000) *Brand Leadership* (New York: The Free Press).

ACNielsen (2000) *Consumer Habits and Attitudes in Argentina* (New York, NY: ACNielsen).

ACNielsen (2002) *Report for the Chilean Market* (www.acnielsen.cl).

Arellano, R. (2000) *Los Estilos de Vida en el Perú. Consumidores & Mercados* (Lima: Consumidores y Mercados).

Audit and Surveys Worldwide (1998) *Pan Latin American Kids Study* (Washington, DC).

Audits and Surveys (1998) *Telecommunications in Latin America* (Washington, DC).

Audits and Surveys (1999) *Telecommunications in Latin America* (Washington, DC).

Audits and Surveys Worldwide (1996) *Los Medios y Mercados de Latinoamerica* (Santiago).

Bianchi, C. and J. Mena, (2004) 'Defending the local market against foreign competitors: The example of Chilean retailers', *International Journal of Retail and Distribution Management*, 32 (10), pp. 495–504.

Burki, S. and G. Perry (eds) (1997) *The Long March: A Reform Agenda for Latin America and the Caribbean in the Next Decade* (Washington, DC: World Bank).

Business Week (1992) June 15.

Business Week (1998) February 9.

Byrne, E. (1994) 'Mexican consumers and their appetites', *Business Mexico*, 4 (54), pp. 16–18.

CEPAL (2000a) 'The new face of urbanization in the cities of Latin America and the Caribbean', *CEPAL News*, 20 (11).

CEPAL (2000b) 'Employment: Aquilles' heel of reforms', *CEPAL News*, 20 (8).

CEPAL (2000c) *La brecha de la equidad en America Latina y el Caribe: Una Segunda Evaluacion* (Santiago, Chile: CEPAL).

Carramengha, P., L. Dougnac and N. Marangoni (1999) 'Evaluating the value of global brands in Latin America', *Marketing in Latin America in the 21st Century* (Santiago, Chile: ESOMAR), pp. 15–30.

Cavusgil, S. T. (1997) 'Measuring the potential of emerging markets: An indexing approach', *Business Horizons*, 14 (1), pp. 87–91.

Cramphorn, M. and J. Caldeiro (1999) 'Effective advertising: Is Ibero America as universal as the rest of the world?', *Marketing in Latin America in the 21st Century* (Santiago, Chile: ESOMAR), pp. 435–57.

de Negri, F. (2003) 'Desempenho comercial das empresas estrangeiras no Brasil na década de 1990', Dissertação de mestrado (MSc dissertation), Instituto de Economia – UNICAMP, Campinas.

de Soto, H. (1989) *The Other Path: Invisible Revolution in the Third World* (London: I. B. Tauris).

de Soto, H., E. Ghersi and M. Ghibellini (1986) *El Otro Sendero* (Lima: Instituto Liberdad y Democracia).

ECLAC (2000) 'The challenging of an aging population', *ECLAC News*, 20 (10).

ECLAC (2000) Market Characteristics.
Economist Intelligence Unit (EIU) (1999) *Consumer Marketing in Latin America* (London: EIU).
Economist Intelligence Unit (EIU) (1999) *Managing Alliances and Acquisitions in Latin America* (London: EIU).
Economist Intelligence Unit (EIU) (2000) 'Beyond Banking', *Business Latin America*, 17 July 2000, 3.
Economist Intelligence Unit (EIU) (2000) *Country Monitor*, 25 December.
Economist Intelligence Unit (EIU) (2005) 'Peru: country background' (www.economist. com/countries/Peru).
El Mercurio (2001) March 24.
Euromonitor (1999–2000) *Consumer International*, 137.
Euromonitor (1999–2000) Consumer International, London.
Gómez, H. (1997) 'The globalization of business in Latin America', *The International Executive*, 39 (2), pp. 225–54.
Ghersi, E. (1997) 'The informal economy in Latin America', *The Cato Journal*, 17 (1), pp. 99–108.
Gouvea, R. (2004) 'Doing business in Brazil: A strategic approach', *Thunderbird International Business Review*, 46 (2), pp. 165–89.
Guthrie, A. (2005) 'Snack-food stores in Mexico grab double-digit annual sales gains', *Wall Street Journal*, 2 February.
Hatten, C. and D. Korsun (2000) 'Latin American Internet penetration, uses and trends', Working Paper (Washington, DC: George Washington University, August).
Hayes, M. (1988–89) 'The U.S. and Latin America: A lost decade?', *Foreign Affairs*, 68 (1), pp. 35–48.
Hofstede, G. (2001) *Culture's Consequences, Comparing Values, Behaviors, Institutions, and Organizations Across Nations* (Thousand Oaks, CA: Sage).
Holcombe, J. (1994) 'Understanding regional income estimates', *Business Latin America*, 5 September.
Holcombe, J. (2000) *Austerity Hits Brazil* (Washington, DC).
IBOPE (2000) *Ciclo de vida do consumidor* (Riode Janeiro).
IMF (2004) World Economic Outlook, April, Washington, DC.
InfoAmerica (2001) January.
Kaufman, S. (2004) 'The style of Brazil', *Visual Store*, 22 September (www.visualstore.com).
Keillor, B. and G. Hult (1999) 'A five-country study of national identity: Implications for international marketing research and practice', *International Marketing Review*, 16 (1), pp. 65–84.
Keller K. (1997) *Strategic Brand Management: Building, Measuring, and Managing Brand Equity* (Englewood Cliffs, NJ Prentice-Hall).
Klein, E. and V. Tokman (2000) 'La estratificación social bajo la tensión en la era de globalización', *Revista de la Cepal*, 72.
La Tercera (1999) 'La nueva clasificacion socio-economica para el consumidor en Chile', September 9.
Landers, W. (2001) 'The impact of Internet and information technology in Latin America', paper presented to the Americas Society, New York, 1 May.
Lara, S. (ed.) (2000) *Dealing with economic insecurity in Latin America* (Washington, DC: World Bank).

Li, F., J. Nicholls, N. Zhou, T. Mandokovic and G. Zhuang (2003) 'A Pacific Rim Debut: Shoppers in China and Chile', *Asia Pacific Journal of Marketing and Logistics*, 15 (1/2), pp. 115–31.

Malkin, E. (2004) 'Mexican retailers unite against Wal-Mart', *The New York Times*, 9 July.

McClintock, C. (1990) 'Washington's anti-narcotics policy: Exacerbating Peru's crisis?', *US Administration Peru Report*, 4 (10), p. 8.

McCoy, T. (2001) *The 2001 Latin American Business Environment: An Assessment*. (Gainesville, FA: Center for Latin American Studies, University of Florida).

Meeker, M., M. Mahaney and F. Cascianelli (2000) *The Latin America Internet Report* (New York: Morgan Stanley Dean Witter).

Meio & Messagem (2001) March 14, page 36.

Meio & Messagem (2001) May 7, page 40.

Mercado (1999) *Radiografia del consumo en la Argentina* (Buenos Aires: Editorial Coyuntura).

Mercado (2000) 'Radiografia del consumo', November.

Mercado (2001) 'El Perfil del Consumidor – Alimentos y Bebidas', 9 October.

MMR (1999) September.

MMR (2000) 'South America draws global retailers', March 20.

Molina, G. (1999) 'Latin American Consumers Beyond Borders', paper of Gallup organization (www.gallup.com/poll/content/login.aspx?ci=9892).

New Strategist (2000) *American Incomes: Demographics of Who Has Money* (Ithaca, NY: New Strategist Publications).

Nicholls, J., F. Li, T. Mandokovic, S. Roslow, and C. Kranendonk (2000) 'US–Chilean mirrors: Shoppers in two countries', *Journal of Consumer Marketing*, 17 (2), pp. 106–19.

Organizacíon Internacional del Trabajo (OIT) (2002) *Panorama Laboral 2002* (Lima: OIT).

Prahalad, C. and K. Lieberthal (1998) 'The end of corporate imperialism', *Harvard Business Review*, 76 (July–August), pp. 69–78.

Reardon, T. and J. Berdegué (2002) 'The rapid rise of supermarkets in Latin America: Challenges and opportunities for development', *Development Policy Review*, 20 (4), pp. 371–88.

Reilly, K. (1999) 'Digital revolution versus Cuban revolution: The internet in Cuba', Working Paper, Carleton University, Ottawa, Canada, December.

Revista Exame (2002) 'Brasil em exame', 27 November São Paolo.

Roberts, D. (2004) 'Tarnished image: Is the world falling out of love with US brands?', *Financial Times*, 30 December, p. 7.

Robles, F., F. Simon and J. Haar (2003) *Winning Strategies for the New Latin Markets* (Prentice-Hall/Financial Times).

Rosenburg, C. (2001) 'A empresa de um rosto só', *Exame*, 18 April.

Ross, J. (2005) 'Wal-Mart invades Mexico', *CounterPunch*, 17 March (www.counterpunch.org).

Ruiz-Velasco, L. (1996) 'La revolución consumista', *AméricaEconomía*, January, pp. 30–2.

Schmidt-Hebbel, K. and L. Serven (1995) 'Fiscal and monetary contraction in Chile: A rational-expectations approach', World Bank Policy Research Working Paper (Washington, DC: World Bank).

Sharma, V. (2002) 'Entry into Latin American BEMs: High or low resource commitment modes?', *International Journal of Commerce and Management*, 12 (1), pp. 41–67.

Soong, R. (2000a) *Shopper Typology in Colombia* (www.zonalatina.com/Z1data 101.htm).

Soong, R. (2000b) *Buying name brands in Argentina* (www.zonalatina.com/Z1data 153.htm).

Sternquist, B. (1997) *International Retailing* (New York, NY: Fairchild Publications).

Strategy Research Corporation (2000) *US Hispanic Market* (Miami, FL: Strategy Research Corporation).

Strategy Research Corporation (2001) *Latin American Market Planning Report* (Miami, FL: Strategy Research Corporation).

Stroudsburg, E. (1999) 'Latin lure: Demographic attracts marketing dollars and focus', *Beverage World*, 31 January–28 February.

Szekely, M. and M. Hilgert (1999) 'The 1990s in Latin America: another decade of persistent inequality', Working Paper no. 235 (Luxembourg, December).

Turner, M. (2001) 'Dream Niche', *US Business Review*, October (www.usbusinessreview.com).

UNCTAD (2004) World Investment Report, Washington, DC: UNCTAD.

United Nations (2004) 'Foreign direct investment in Latin America and the Caribbean' (www.eclac.cl/publicaciones/DesarrolloProductivo/6/LCG2226/Foreign Rep2003.pdf).

Vasquez-Parraga, A., R. Felix and A. Borders (2004) 'Rationale and strategies of Latin American companies entering, maintaining or leaving US markets', *Journal of Business and Industrial Marketing*, 19 (6), pp. 359–71.

Walker, C. (1995) 'The Global Middle Class', *American Demographics*, September.

Wall Street Journal (1995) January 11, page 2.

Wall Street Journal Americas (2003) October 27.

Williamson, J. (2003) 'An agenda for restarting growth and reform'. in P.-P. Kuczynski and J. Williamson (eds), *After the Washington Consensus: Restarting Growth and Reform in Latin America* (Washington, DC: Institute for International Economics), pp. 1–19.

Wodon, Q. (2000) 'Poverty and policy in Latin America and the Caribbean', World Bank Working Paper no. 457 (Washington, DC: World Bank).

World Bank (2000) *Entering the 21st Century: World Development Report* (Washington, DC: World Bank).

World Trade (1999) 'Argentina's consumer market modifies', February.

Zuin, V. (2004) *Business strategies of informal micro entrepreneurs in Lima, Peru*, Discussion Paper 150, Decent Research Programme (Geneva: International Institute for Labour Studies).

Index